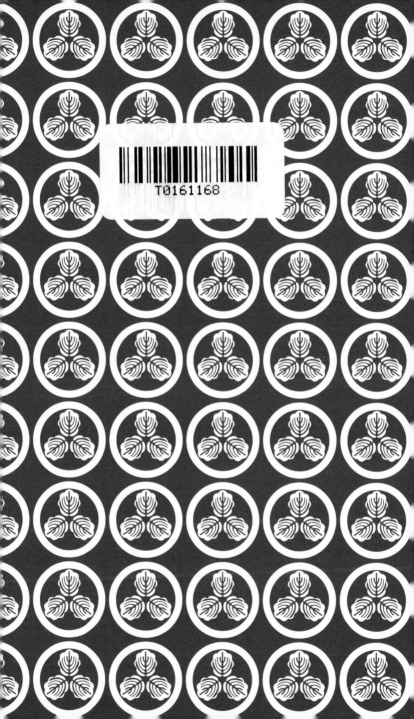

WARRIOR
WISDOM

WARRIOR
WISDOM

WARRIOR WISDOM

KAZUMI TABATA

TUTTLE Publishing

Tokyo | Rutland, Vermont | Singapore

Published by Tuttle Publishing, an imprint of Periplus Editions (HK) Ltd.

www.tuttlepublishing.com

Copyright © 2013 Kazumi Tabata

Library of Congress Cataloging-in-Publication Data

Tabata, Kazumi, 1943-
  Warrior wisdom / Kazumi Tabata.
    p. cm.
  Includes bibliographical references.
  ISBN 978-4-8053-1271-1 (hardcover)
  1. Martial arts--Japan--Philosophy. I. Title.
  GV1100.77.A2T34 2013
  796.8--dc23

                                    201204
2034

Distributed by

North America, Latin America & Europe
Tuttle Publishing
364 Innovation Drive
North Clarendon, VT 05759-9436 U.S.A.
Tel: 1 (802) 773-8930
Fax: 1 (802) 773-6993
info@tuttlepublishing.com
www.tuttlepublishing.com

Japan
Tuttle Publishing
Yaekari Building, 3rd Floor
5-4-12 Osaki
Shinagawa-ku
Tokyo 141 0032
Tel: (81) 3 5437-0171
Fax: (81) 3 5437-0755
sales@tuttle.co.jp
www.tuttle.co.jp

Asia Pacific
Berkeley Books Pte. Ltd.
61 Tai Seng Avenue #02-12
Singapore 534167
Tel: (65) 6280-1330
Fax: (65) 6280-6290
inquiries@periplus.com.sg
www.periplus.com

First edition
17 16 15 14 13   10 9 8 7 6 5 4 3 2 1

1302RP

Printed in China

TUTTLE PUBLISHING® is a registered trademark of Tuttle Publishing, a division of Periplus Editions (HK) Ltd.

ISBN 978-4-8053-1271-1

CONTENTS

BOOK THREE
The Tactics of Shokatsu Komei:
The Art of War

BOOK FOUR
The Nature of the Martial Arts

BOOK FIVE
Mind Control and the Method

BOOK SIX
Humor and Laughter

BOOK SEVEN
Image Reading

BOOK EIGHT
Wisdom and Tactics

FOREWORD

The third book of my favorite Tactics series by Shihan Kazumi Tabata has finally arrived and it is my great pleasure to endorse this best selling series.

Shihan Tabata and I are fellow pupils and descendants of Sensei Isao Obata, founder and first Chief Director of Japan Karate-do Federation.

While I am in the business field, Shihan Tabata was dispatched overseas by Sensei Isao Obata to promote Karate. Over the years, Shihan Tabata has been teaching Karate at universities, mastered esoteric learning, awakened to the state of enlightenment to apply what he learned to the real world, and established a whole worldview that is different from the past books written about martial arts.

The soul of martial arts exists in a world you can come to understand only after you reach the mysterious esoteric learning of the East. This book completes the series that has moved many of its readers. This series is well constructed and readers may come to understand this world of enlightenment as they read forward. The accomplishments the author attained through training and effort shines brilliantly throughout the series.

This book covers everything thoroughly yet simply, from immovable heart, *fudo-shin* (the universe and I are the same), world of the nothingness (*mu*) and the emptiness (*ku*), boundary of inner strength, to enlightenment of ancestors including classic texts. I feel privileged that I met this book. Readers who have all the books of this series can keep them over a lifetime and find new frontiers with every new read. This book not only guides you through life but also establishes wealth in your heart by connecting you with various worlds. I am sure it can help you break through the walls that appear in your life.

I am impressed and confident that these books will be read by those who come after us. I am honored to live in the same generation with Shihan Tabata. With confidence and pride, I truly recommend this book to keep by your side over your lifetime.

Satoshi Nishitani
Descendant of Isao Obata
President, Kawaden Corporation
Chief Director, Japan Businessman Karate-do Federation
(Renmei)

AUTHOR'S PREFACE

A turbulent time can be a time of opportunity. *Heiho* (strategy) can serve as practical criteria for making judgments. Such criteria must be based on facts.

Reality is uncertain and situations change. Therefore, our criteria should be based on what happened in the past.

During the tumultuous times of war, when warriors played every trick imaginable on each other—engaged in diplomatic maneuvering, pressed their demands, and achieved grandiose goals—clever fighters outsmarted their opponents. That was when *Heiho* was born. The book of *Heiho* captures the essence of classic military tactics designed to win.

The essence of military tactics, developed many centuries ago, is still relevant today, providing us with new insight and captivating information.

I would be honored if this book could be of any help to you in uncovering the clues to understanding the essence of reality.

Gasshou
Kazumi Tabata

Chi E

Bu-kei (*Military Strategy*)

BOOK ONE

The Art of War By Sun Tsu

The Art of War by Sun Tsu is the most widely read among *bukei-nanasho* (seven books on military strategy). This book is known to be written by Sun Tsu, a military strategist who lived more than 2,500 years ago. Sun Tsu was a military commander who served Koryo, the king of Go (514–496 BC). This book is based on the following premises: one should win without fighting; one should not fight when prospects of winning are poor; and one should utilize a weak force to overcome a powerful force. The book is about pursuing this military strategy.

This section will attempt to convey the gist of Sun Tsu's work.

About Sun Tsu

One day, Koryo, the king of Go, requested Sun Tsu to train soldiers. One hundred and eighty beautiful ladies of the Imperial Court were recruited and divided into two groups. Two of the king's favorite women were appointed as group leaders. Sun Tsu had all the women carry a pike. He instructed them to look at the chest when he said "front," the left hand when he said "left," the right hand when he said "right," and the back when he said "back." He explained the procedure and repeated this exercise. Once he started beating the drum and said "right," the women began to laugh. Sun Tsu said, "It was my fault that the women did not understand my instructions." After explaining how to do it and repeating the exercise again, he gave a command once more. When he said "left" as he beat the drum, the women started laughing again and failed to carry out the command. He said, "The first time was my fault, but this time, it is different. It is the group leaders' fault that the command is not being relayed, despite the fact that the women all understand what the command means," and attempted to strike down the two leaders with a sword. When the king tried to intervene, Sun Tsu explained as follows and struck down the two female leaders: "I am the commander. When the commander is fulfilling his military duties, he may not always be able to follow the king's orders." Sun Tsu then appointed two other beautiful ladies as their successors. When he gave a command, the women carried it out in an orderly manner. Sun Tsu said to the king, "Training of soldiers has been completed. If ordered, the soldiers will jump into the water or fire. Please give it a try." The king replied, "There is no need for that," and recognized Sun Tsu's exceptional ability as strategist and hired him as military commander.

Shikei (*Basic Planning*)

Shikei (Basic Planning)

Shikei refers to basic planning needed to initiate a move. This chapter discusses the five criteria for winning a battle, in an attempt to prevent frivolous wars.

Basic Military Power

The outcome of war can determine the fate of people and the nation's existence. Whether or not to go to war must be carefully considered. In order to win a war, five basic conditions should be taken into account: path, heaven, land, leadership, and law.

Path refers to principles or policies. Only when intentions of the people and their sovereign coincide, the people will be willing to share their fate with the sovereign without being afraid of danger. This is a prerequisite to following the path to victory.

Heaven refers to situations or timing. This condition includes weather, season, occasion, and timing.

Land refers to environmental factors. This condition includes geographical factors such as distance, ruggedness, width, and height.

Leadership refers to a leader's qualifications. This condition includes a leader's virtuous qualities such as ingenuity, loyalty, benevolence, courage, and dignity.

Law refers to organization, discipline, and equipment. This condition includes military structure, discipline, and readiness in terms of equipment.

In order to determine if the above five conditions are met, you should examine your prospects by considering the seven comparisons below.

Which side has a better political system?

Which side has better commanders?

Which side enjoys more favorable situational and geographical factors?

Which side enforces the law more thoroughly?
Which side is stronger militarily?
Which side has better-trained soldiers?
Which side has a fairer system of reward and punishment?

When conditions are favorable to you, you must solidify your position by reinforcing the advantageous factors. You should also put more effort into enhancing the basic conditions. Since the basic conditions are constantly changing, you should be able to adapt yourself to any change in circumstances. Your response to the situation should change accordingly. There is no need to adhere to basic rules. If conditions are right, you will win; otherwise, you will lose. Do not fight when prospects of winning are poor.

To Fight is to Deceive

Flexibility is required in a battle. The key to victory is to focus on the enemy's weaknesses and to take them by surprise.

1. Move closer while pretending to be moving away.
2. Hide your competence and feign incompetence.
3. Make something essential appear unnecessary.
4. Move away while pretending to be moving closer.
5. Lure your opponent by falsely showing that conditions are advantageous to him.
6. Defeat your adversary by creating confusion.
7. When things are going well for the enemy, withdraw and reposition yourself.
8. Avoid a head-on clash with powerful enemies.
9. Exhaust your opponent by infuriating him.
10. Throw the enemy off guard by keeping a low profile.
11. When your opponent is at rest, cause a commotion to exhaust him.
12. When the enemy demonstrates solidarity, break them apart.

A good strategy is to exploit the enemy's weaknesses and take them by surprise. A strategy should not be predetermined in advance; rather, it should be adapted to changing circumstances.

Prospects

- Whether or not you will win depends on your prospects.
- Those who do not carefully examine their chances of winning will not win.
- If your prospects are excellent, you will win.
- When conditions are right, you will win; when conditions are not right, you will lose.
- When conditions are unfavorable, you cannot expect to win.
- Avoid fighting when your prospects are poor.

Tactics

When devising military tactics, plan for a quick war with meticulous preparations, which can achieve full effects with minimal sacrifice.

Short war
Since the cost of war can be enormous, you should strive to end the war quickly. Why do you need to end it quickly?

In a prolonged battle, troops must be mobilized on a large scale to provide logistic support for weapons and soldiers, and long-distance transportation of supplies will be needed.

An all-out war requires massive military spending domestically and internationally. Entertaining diplomatic envoys and supplying military goods, vehicles, and weapons will cost an enormous amount of money each day. A protracted war will not only exhaust troops and undermine their morale, but also make them prone to mistakes. Furthermore, such a war may ruin the national finances.

Depletion of national wealth will give other nations an opportunity to take advantage of the situation. When national wealth is depleted, no wise men will be able to fix the problem. There are successful examples of short war, but there are no such examples of prolonged war. Lengthy military campaigns will not bring any benefits to the nation.

Procurement
War can ruin national power because it requires long-distance transportation of military goods. This can place a heavy burden on people, cause inflation, and impoverish the nation. People will suffer from heavy taxation, leading to exhaustion of national power. Seventy percent of national income will go toward mili-

tary spending, and sixty percent of the national budget will be lost due to military losses. A wise monarch avoids repeated transportation of additional weapons, troops, and goods long distances. He procures equipment in his home country and other goods locally in the enemy territory. Food procured locally in the hostile territory is worth as much as twenty times the food imported from the home country, saving transportation costs.

Compensation gained as a result of war is acceptable, but looting of the houses of local people to procure goods is unacceptable. Goods must be purchased at a fair price. When in the enemy territory, do not lay even a finger on the belongings of local people. Speak to them politely and calmly; do not strike or intimidate them.

Selling and buying should be done fairly. Return borrowed items. Pay for any damage done to people's property. Do not damage agricultural crops. Do not terrorize women. Do not abuse prisoners of war. The act of looting in the enemy territory will result in the loss of support of local people. Strict discipline among troops will earn the trust of local people.

Victory enhances your power

- Provoke the feeling of antagonism toward the enemy among your troops.
- What drives soldiers to take up arms is the will to fight.
- The will to fight can be heightened by reward.
- Soldiers need to be assured that they will be recompensed for their achievements.
- Soldiers who render distinguished service should be the first to be rewarded.
- When you seize the enemy's equipment, switch the banners to yours and have your soldiers utilize the equipment. Prisoners of war should be treated kindly and incorporated into your military force so that winning a battle makes you even stronger.

- A war must be won. A protracted conflict should be avoided and a battle should be finished swiftly. Only a commander who understands this reality is qualified to be entrusted with the nation's security and people's lives.

Ki-saku (*Trick*)

Boko (Strategic Offense)

War is not an end in itself; the means is the end. The best victory is to win without fighting.

The best victory

- The best victory is to force your opponent to surrender without harming him.
- The best strategy is to force your opponent to surrender without fighting him.
- Forcing your adversary to surrender by defeating him is the second best strategy.
- Even if you win 100 out of 100 battles, it is not the best strategy.
- The best tactic is to contain your adversary by seeing through his intentions in advance.
- The second best tactic is to break up the enemy's alliance to isolate them.
- The third best tactic is to engage in battle.
- The fourth best tactic is to attack the enemy's castle. This should be the last resort, when everything else fails.
- Attacking the castle entails elaborate preparations and sacrifice of soldiers. Your efforts may prove futile. A capable military commander can make the enemy surrender without resorting to force. He can capture their castle without attacking it.
- Secondly, the commander can defeat the enemy by fighting a short battle.
- Thirdly, the commander can prevail by gaining the support of the enemy without harming them.
- Fourthly, the commander can pull off a perfect victory while preserving the strength of armed forces.

Military tactics
- When your military strength is ten times as powerful as the enemy's, encircle the enemy.
- When your military strength is five times as powerful as the enemy's, attack the enemy.
- When your military strength is twice as powerful as the enemy's, split up the enemy.
- When your military strength is the same as the enemy's, make an all-out effort.
- When your military strength is inferior to the enemy's, withdraw your troops.
- Do not fight a losing battle.

Those who fight without any regard to the above principles will become easy prey for the enemy. Retreat should be a means to prepare for counter-attack.

The Meddlesome Sovereign
When the military commander and the sovereign are on good terms, the country will be powerful; when they are on bad terms, the country will weaken. Unnecessary interference in military affairs by the sovereign may lead to a military crisis.

The following are the examples of unnecessary interference by the monarch:
1. Ordering troops to advance or retreat when it is inappropriate to do so. The military will be shackled by such orders.
2. Interfering in military affairs without having intimate knowledge of the internal workings of the military. This will plant the seeds of distrust in the armed forces.

When the monarch creates confusion and distrust among military personnel, other nations may take advantage of the situation and attack. Unnecessary interference by the monarch is a suicidal act.

Know Yourself and your Adversary

Knowing your adversary and yourself will ensure victory in 100 battles.

Requirements for victory:

1. You must have the ability to determine whether or not to fight after assessing the enemy's military power.
2. You must be able to fight according to your military strength.
3. The sovereign and his subjects should pursue the same goal.
4. You must have the ability to make thorough preparations and take advantage of the enemy's vulnerability.
5. The military commander must be competent. For the commander to be competent, the monarch should not interfere with the commander's control.
6. Victory is certain when you know your enemy and yourself.
7. The odds of winning are 50-50 when you know yourself but not your enemy.
8. Defeat is inevitable when you know neither yourself nor your enemy.

Gunkei (Military Format)

The top priority in battle is to launch an attack with minimal effort by finding the enemy's weak points after building an unbeatable defense.

It is foolish to rely on soldiers' valor on the battlefield. *Gunkei* (format) is useless if it is fixed. Defense is useless if it is fixed. A great feat can be accomplished only when you are able to adapt your tactics to the enemy like water.

In the past, skillful warriors prevailed without flaunting their military acumen, and no one praised their valor. Such victory was pursued by good fighters.

Waiting for the Enemy to Collapse

An expert warrior in the past strengthened his position first, and waited for his opponent to start revealing his flaws.

Whether or not you remain undefeated depends on the state of your troops. Whether or not you have a chance of winning depends on the state of enemy troops.

Skilled fighters can enhance their invincibility, but they cannot create invincible conditions.

Even when victory is expected, victory is not always certain. Fortifying defense and attacking the enemy's weaknesses will not guarantee victory; however, at least it can help strengthen your position to remain unbeaten.

A skillful fighter's strategy is to wait for his adversary to start revealing his failings. If your defense is flawless, the enemy will not be able to strike. If the enemy seems faultless, focus on reinforcing your troops and avoid carrying out unnecessary attacks. Make sure to strengthen defense before launching an attack.

Offense and Defense

When conditions required for victory do not exist, reinforce your defense. When the chance of winning is high, go on the offensive.

When you are on the defensive, you are losing. When you are on the offensive, you are winning. When on the defensive, good warriors preserve troop strength to guard against the enemy. When on the offensive, good warriors attack swiftly without giving their opponents a chance to defend themselves. By doing this, such warriors can secure complete victory without suffering any damage.

A competent commander does not make a mistake in determining whether to go on the offensive or defensive. Caution is important, but excessive caution may lead to overemphasis on defense. Conversely, excessive boldness may lead to inattentiveness.

The Best Victory

A victory that is obvious to everyone is not the best victory. A victory that draws public praise is not the best victory. A person who can lift a hair is not considered mighty. A person who can see the sun and moon is not considered to have keen eyesight. A person who can hear the sound of thunder is not considered to have acute hearing. Even an ordinary person can do such things naturally. This constitutes the publicly-praised best victory.

Skillful fighters in the past won a battle naturally. Even when they won, their ingenuity was inconspicuous, and their valor was not applauded. Such warriors always prevailed. Every move they made was successful, making no significant errors. The reason for their success was that they chose to fight those who were destined to lose.

Good fighters place their troops in a position that guarantees invincibility. They never fail to detect a flaw in the enemy's move. As can be seen, only those who are fully prepared to claim victory will succeed. A good monarch first undertakes a political reform.

He then strictly enforces the law to make preparations needed to secure victory.

Those who scramble to seize a chance to win after going into battle will suffer defeat.

Four Factors that Determine the Outcome of Battle

The outcome of battle is determined by land area, size of resources, population size, and military power. When the ratio of total power between your country and the enemy nation is 500 to 1, victory will be certain. Any commander can then win without much effort.

Advance calculation and comprehensive assessment are needed to ensure victory; otherwise, defeat is inevitable. Like stopped-up water rapidly falling into a deep ravine, you can overwhelm your opponents.

Heisei (Status of the Military)

Masterly warriors place emphasis on giving momentum to military organization. Momentum can double or even triple the power of an organization. To fight is to skillfully combine *ki* (unconventional) and *sei* (conventional) to gain momentum in battle. There are an infinite number of such combinations. The key to victory is to apply such combinations to achieve military objectives.

Military formation, control, conventional and unconventional methods

In order to control large units as if they were small units, reorganize the units by dividing them into proper groups. To have the large units fight in unity like small units, firmly establish the chain of command.

We use a stone to break an egg. Likewise, to ensure victory, we need to use *mi* (substance), which represents effective military power, to attack *kyo* (void), which represents weak points. A commander skilled at using *ki* (unconventional methods) is able to successfully adapt his tactics to the particular time and situation. Such tactics will be infinite like the flow of a big river and endless like heaven and earth. Such a commander disappears and reemerges like the sun and the moon. He vanishes and reappears like four seasons. Such flexible tactics are needed for the entire military to gain the upper hand over the enemy.

There are only five basic musical scales, but an infinite number of variations is possible when they are combined. Also, colors and flavors can be combined to create an unlimited number of variations. Likewise, there are a countless number of possible combinations of *ki* (conventional) and *sei* (unconventional), both of which constitute military tactics. Since the possibilities are endless, no one can ever know all of them.

Momentum

Gain momentum rather than acquiring useless knowledge. When water is held back, it will eventually form a torrent and wash away boulders. There lies the momentum.

A raptor crushes its prey with one stroke. There lies the explosive force.

When a bow is drawn fully, an accumulated force will be released as momentum, instantly transforming itself into explosive force. Such an accumulated force is destructive.

Control

When there is confusion and chaos on the battlefield, order can quickly turn into disorder. Whether there will be order or disorder depends on control.

Bravery can change into cowardice. Whether there will be bravery or cowardice depends on momentum. Strength can easily be transformed into weakness. Whether there will be strength or weakness depends on circumstances.

Warriors skilled at strategizing pressure their opponents to make a move. Such warriors put out the bait to lure their opponents, who will be tempted by a chance to benefit themselves. Once they take the bait, such warriors waste no time in overwhelming them with powerful military strength.

When there is confusion on the battlefield, do not allow soldiers to fall into disarray. Even when there is chaos on the battlefield, never let your guard down.

Seek Momentum Instead of Assistance

Logs and stones are stationary when placed on a flat surface. When they are placed on a slope, they will start moving naturally. Angular objects remain still; round objects roll over. To fight with momentum is to let the round stones roll swiftly into the bottom of a canyon.

Masterful fighters stress the importance of gaining momentum. They do not expect much from each soldier; rather, they value the momentum of the armed forces as a whole. They focus on uniting the entire military and building up momentum.

Seek momentum instead of assistance. Rather than asking for help, swim with the current of the times.

Substance and Void

Like the flow of water, the war situation does not take on a particular shape. To gain advantage in battle, you need to take control and manipulate your adversary at will.

Be the first to arrive on the scene. Break up enemy forces. Avoid powerful enemies and attack weak points. To fight is to focus on substance and void.

Control

Good warriors strive to take control of the situation.

First, entice the enemy by making them believe that the situation is in their favor. To prevent the enemy from readying themselves for war, keep them from believing that the situation is against them.

When your opponent is at rest, do whatever is necessary to confuse and exhaust him. When your opponent is eating well, block the food supply to starve him. When your opponent is calm, initiate a scheme to distress him. When your opponent is on the offensive, outsmart him by launching an unexpected attack.

You will be able to fight with composure if you arrive first on the battlefield, waiting for the enemy's arrival. Conversely, you will struggle if you arrive late on the scene to confront enemy forces awaiting you.

To fight is to turn the tables. To ensure victory, strike the enemy at places where defense is vulnerable. When on the defensive, defend spots that are difficult for the enemy to attack.

When on an expedition to the hostile territory, choose a route free of enemy forces. When confronted by good offense, it may be difficult to know where to defend. When confronted by good defense, it may be difficult to know where to attack. To take control is to be able to implement this strategy at will.

When you do not want to fight, make your opponent unable to fight. Use unconventional tactics to throw him into confusion. Conversely, when you want to fight, strike at places your opponent cannot ignore.

To gain control, your opponent's power must be shifted toward you. Take control of the situation by using your opponent's power, rather than resorting to force. War is a struggle for control. When troops lose control after being forced to act defensively, they will lose freedom of action and suffer defeat.

Convergence and Dispersion

The size of armed forces is not an absolute measurement of strength; what matters is the condition of your troops and enemy forces.

When the opposition's next move is not known, your troops will have to be stretched thin to cover vast regions. Conversely, this means that when the size of your troops is large, you can disperse enemy troops by concealing your next move.

If enemy troops are forced to stay in one place with the possibility of being attacked from any direction, they have no choice but to split up.

If you can follow the opposition's every step without allowing them to know your next move, this will force the other side to divert their resources. Once enemy troops are scattered, you will have fewer soldiers to confront.

When the front is reinforced, the rear becomes vulnerable. When the rear is reinforced, the front becomes vulnerable. When all sides are reinforced, all sides become vulnerable.

Victory is the result of human efforts; victory is not the result of a natural course of action. Even when you are outnumbered and eclipsed by enemy forces, you can disable them through the tactics of convergence and dispersion. You can turn the tables by having your troops converge while at the same time dispersing enemy forces.

Knowing where and when fighting will take place before the enemy does ensures victory, even after travelling for 1,000 *ri* (250 miles).

Lack of this knowledge makes it impossible for soldiers to cooperate. Such information is crucial especially when you are on a military expedition.

Being Able to Change Flexibly

There are four requirements for victory. That is to say, there are four ways to gather information about the enemy.

1.   Examine the war situation to assess who is stronger.
2.   Entice the enemy into making a move.
3.   Provoke the enemy into action to identify the geographically vital spots that can decide their fate.
4.   Cause a skirmish to determine the strong and weak points of the enemy.

In times of war, it is of utmost importance to never allow the opposition to know your war plans. With this policy in place, even if enemy spies infiltrated into your troops on the battlefield, they would not find anything valuable. Even if commanders of enemy forces were ingenuous, they would not be able to attack and prevail.

Ordinary people may have difficulty understanding the fact that adjusting war plans to the condition of the enemy will bring victory. Ordinary people may eventually find out that success is attributed to the military strategy adopted by troops. However, it may be hard for them to understand that rejection of inflexible plans and adoption of flexible attitudes have resulted in success. It is important to remember that plans can be modified in countless ways depending on whom you are fighting with.

It is wrong to repeat the same strategy that was successful before. You should maintain your mobility.

Like Water

War plans should be like the flow of water. Water flows from a high place to a low place. Water lacks definite shape; likewise, war lacks definite plans. Avoid attacking the enemy's strong points and strike them at their weak points.

Good military tactics is to win by adapting to the enemy's war plans. It is comparable to the changing laws of nature. The five classical elements of wood, fire, earth, gold, and water interact with each other to change everything in nature. Seasonal transitions, change in daylight hours, waxing and waning of the moon. These are all fluid. Water changes its shape to fit any container. War plans must be the same. They should be fluid.

Hayate (*A swift wind*)

Gunso (Preparations for War)

Gunso refers to preparations for war. In order to succeed in a battle, you need to deceive the adversary nation and disturb their judgment. For this to work, you must act, respond, and change under favorable circumstances.

One of the requirements for victory is to maintain morale. Combine *sei* (conventional) and *ki* (unconventional), and movement and stillness to win effectively. When you are on the defensive under favorable circumstances, assume an imposing posture and do not let your opponents get the upper hand. When on the offensive, attack swiftly and decisively.

More Haste, Less Speed

A war begins when a military commander organizes armed forces under the order of the sovereign. He then positions his troops to confront the enemy. The difficult part is how to fight the subsequent battle and create conditions that will bring victory. Give a false sense of security to the other side by intentionally taking a detour, so that you can arrive at the destination before the enemy and turn disadvantages into advantages. However, it may be difficult to pull this off.

Depart for the destination later than enemy troops to trick them into thinking they are safe. Lack of interruption by the other side should enable your troops to arrive early. Like this, do something unconventional to throw your opponents off guard and attack. The psychological impact of such an unexpected move is even bigger.

Creating the conditions needed for victory entails danger. Having to transport heavy equipment and deploy the entire armed forces for combat at the same time may make it difficult to keep up with enemy troops. On the other hand, rushing to the destination without proper equipment will leave behind the transportation units. If soldiers are forced to march to the battlefield day and night without sufficient sleep, there may be disastrous consequences. Only the strongest soldiers will make it to the combat zone, leaving behind weak ones. Only one-tenth of the soldiers will arrive on the battleground to fight the enemy.

When you are on a 50-*ri* (125 mile) expedition, only half of troops will make it to the battlefield, and the leader of the first unit to arrive on the scene will be slain. Likewise, when you are on a 30-*ri* (75 mile) expedition, you will be forced to fight with only two-thirds of your troops.

Your troops will lose without the support of logistics units. Your troops will lose without food and other supplies.

To strategize is to deceive. Techniques of deception will emerge from careful observation of the laws of nature. If you want to shrink something, stretch it first. If you want to weaken something, strengthen it first. If you want to take something, give first.

It is difficult to succeed in diplomatic negotiations if you are not current on the latest developments in other nations. It is impossible to advance your troops if you are not familiar with the terrain of the adversary nation. It is impossible to take advantage of favorable geographical conditions without a local guide.

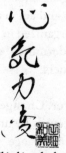

Shin-ki-ryoku-hen
(Shin: Heart; Ki: Spirit; Ryoku: Strength; Hen: Change)

The objective of strategic operations is to deceive. To deceive your opponents, proceed under favorable circumstances. Troop strength should be adapted to changing situations.

A strategic operation must be carried out like a gale; be quiet like a forest; attack like a raging fire; remain absolutely still like a mountain; roar like thunder after disappearing into the dark night. This is how a strategic operation should be undertaken.

To fight is to attack the enemy's villages, seize manpower, and capture physical resources controlled by the enemy. To achieve these goals, any action you take should be based on accurate judgment. Give your opponents a false sense of security by doing something unconventional. Be the first to implement offensive strategy. By meeting the requirements for victory, you will win.

Managing Large Numbers of People

According to ancient books on the art of war, when trying to control a large number of soldiers, commanders used drums to signal because it was difficult for troops to hear oral instructions. They are said to have used banners as signs to make it easier for soldiers who were too far out to see well. The purpose of using these objects was to unite the ears and eyes of soldiers. To unify massive troops, do not allow self-serving behavior. Make sure that cowards do not run away. This is the secret to managing a large number of people. An organization can function properly only when people obey orders and act in an orderly fashion. When confronted with troops organized in such a way, the morale of enemy forces will be undermined, effectively disturbing the minds of enemy commanders.

Mind, ki (Energy), Power, Change

A capable commander prevails by understanding morale, psychology, military power, and change.

1. Morale – People are usually filled with energy in the morning. By noon, people become somewhat lethargic

and try to get some rest in the afternoon. The same is true for the morale of soldiers. Good combatants avoid fighting when the morale of their adversaries is high, waiting for a chance to strike when the morale is low. This is called taking control of *ki* .

2. Mind – Prepare your troops for a battle while waiting for the enemy to fall into disorder. During that period, keep a low profile and wait for the other side to make a move. This is called understanding the "mind" of the enemy.

3. Military power – Station your troops at an advantageous location and wait for adversaries traveling from distant places. During that period, take sufficient rest and wait for your opponents to become exhausted. Keep your troops well fed and wait for the enemy to be starved. This is called sapping the "power" of the enemy.

4. Change – Deploy powerful troops and prepare for a battle. Avoid a head-on clash with the enemy on the offensive. This is called taking control of the "change."

Basic Rules to Follow

There are basic rules to be followed and to be avoided in battle. There are two sides to everything. You should be able to discern the different sides. Try to identify the underlying laws of progress; it will be the first step toward victory.

1. Do not attack enemy troops stationed on higher ground.
2. Do not attack enemy troops positioned with their backs against a hill.
3. Do not pursue opponents taking flight intentionally.
4. Do not attack adversaries full of aggression.
5. Do not jump on soldiers acting as a decoy.
6. Do not stand in the way of opponents who are on their way home.
7. Before surrounding enemy troops, make sure to secure an escape route.

8.   Do not approach adversaries driven into a corner.

Opponents without a way out may launch a frenzied counterattack. This can cause significant damage. The same can be said for personal relationships. When an adult is driven into a corner, he may eventually strike back fiercely and viciously. When a child is driven into a corner, he may choose to take his life.

Kyu-hen (Nine Changes)

Kyu-hen refers to adaptability in war situations. Even if you are armed with knowledge of great principles, the knowledge alone will not be sufficient to secure victory. As a military commander, you need to know how to respond flexibly. Adherence to inflexible thinking will inevitably result in failure. Success requires a flexible, well-balanced way of thinking.

Five rules commanders should follow on the battle-ground

1. There are paths that should not be taken. Do not station your troops at a disadvantageous location.
2. There are enemies that should not be attacked. In a region under the influence of multiple nations, diplomatic negotiations should be emphasized.
3. There are castles that should not be besieged. Once you have penetrated deep into the hostile territory, avoid lingering in the same spot for a long time.
4. There are territories that should not be seized. If unable to move freely after being surrounded by enemy forces, use a clever scheme to find a way out.
5. There are orders that should not be obeyed. When in a life-threatening situation, fighting courageously is the only option. When a golden opportunity is presented before their eyes, people will jump at it without much thought. There are benefits that should not be enjoyed.

Advantages and Disadvantages

A wise man will weigh both advantages and disadvantages when devising a strategy. When analyzing advantages of a plan, you should also take its disadvantages into account. Likewise, when analyzing disadvantages of a plan, you should also take its advantages into account.

1. In order to force your adversary to surrender, inflict damage on him.
2. In order to deplete the national wealth of the enemy, purposefully cause a disturbance to exhaust them.
3. In order to win over the support of your opponents, lure them into your camp by offering some benefits.
4. In a war, do not simply wish that the enemy will not attack; rather, make it difficult for the enemy to attack. Reinforce defense to deprive your adversaries of a chance to counterattack.
5. Abandon wishful thinking and be ready for all types of weather.

Five Dangerous Situations for Commanders
Since ancient times, there are five reasons or causes for the demise of the military and its commanders.

1. Sheer desperation can result in death on the battlefield. When it is time to retreat, you must withdraw.
2. Do not make a frantic attempt to survive. You may end up being captured.
3. Do not lose your temper or become irritable. You may play into the hands of the enemy.
4. Do not insist on being morally right. You may end up responding to provocation by your opponents.
5. Do not be too sympathetic toward common people. You may suffer emotional breakdown.

The most important quality of a commander is the ability to judge comprehensively. The commander's duty is to encourage his subordinates to make frantic efforts without being desperate himself. Do not be too fastidious. Fastidiousness can be a weakness. Every action will set off a reaction.

Ko-gun (March)

The prerequisite for advancing your troops to the combat zone is to become familiar with the topography of the region and alter your fighting methods accordingly. Do not neglect to examine the status of the enemy. Do not overlook even seemingly trivial phenomena. Every phenomenon has its cause and reason. Analyze it with utmost caution. When the condition of the enemy is known, prepare your troops for a battle, being mindful of the situation of the other side. Do not rush recklessly.

Fighting According to the Terrain

1. When fighting in the mountainous terrain – When marching in the mountainous region, move along the valley. Position your troops on higher ground where you can have an unobstructed view. When enemy forces are positioned on higher ground, do not strike. Think of a way to lure them into action.

2. When fighting in the river region – When your adversaries are crossing the river to strike, launch an attack after half of them have reached the shore. When taking the offensive, stay away from the riverbank where your footing is not secure. Engage in combat away from the riverbank. When your troops have to be stationed near the riverbank, choose higher ground where you can have an unobstructed view. Do not fight with opponents positioned upstream when you are located downstream.

3. When fighting in wetlands – When crossing marshy areas where your footing is not firm, move as fast as you can. An attack by the opposition can have devastating effects. When fighting in wetlands, take advantage of swamps and bushes and position yourself in front of

trees. Fight there to turn the tide in your favor.

4.   When fighting in flatlands – To deploy your troops, choose a flat area with lowland in the front and highland in the rear. To station your troops, choose an area with highland on either side and in the rear, which allows free movement. The above is the stratagem to take advantage of the terrain.

5.   Choose higher ground rather than lower ground to deploy your troops.

6.   Be sure to closely manage your soldiers' health. Choose a place with sufficient sunlight rather than a humid spot in the shade. This will raise soldiers' spirits, thereby avoiding health-related issues and energizing them.

7.   When your troops need to be positioned on a hill or embankment, pick a southeastern location, which is geographically favorable. This will enable you to run a campaign to your advantage.

8.   If water levels are rising due to rainfall upriver, wait until the current is manageable to cross. Do not rush.

Terrain to Avoid

1.   A ravine with precipitous cliffs on both sides and a stream inbetween.

2.   A deeply depressed area surrounded by precipices in all four directions.

3.   An area surrounded by steep cliffs on three sides, with a narrow passage on one side. Such an area is difficult to escape.

4.   A place with dense vegetation, where communication with fellow soldiers is difficult and movement is restricted.

5.   A low-lying region where movement is restricted.

6.   A mountainous region with rugged terrain.

When your troops enter such terrain while marching, search the area carefully to ensure that no enemy is lurking. Do not approach such terrain if discovered in advance. Conversely, attempt to drive your adversaries into such terrain. It is important to give a sense of security to your soldiers to boost their morale.

Anticipating Movements of the Enemy

Be cautious if enemy forces remain unusually silent as you approach them. They may be plotting against you. You should assume that they are enjoying natural advantages or some other factors favorable to them.

If enemy troops stationed at a distance are being provocative without physically approaching you, they are trying to tempt you into action.

If opposition forces leave a geographically favorable location and position themselves on flatland, you should assume that the new location gives them some kind of advantage.

Swinging of tree branches is a sign that enemy forces have made inroads into your territory.

Traps laid in a tussock indicate that your adversaries are trying to contain advancement of your troops.

When birds suddenly fly away, it is a sign that soldiers are lying in ambush. When beasts dash off in surprise, it is a sign that there are commando units. When there are clouds of dust high in the air, it is a sign that enemy tanks are invading. When there are clouds of dust hovering low, it is a sign that infantry units are approaching. When there are narrow columns of dust in the air, it is a sign that enemy troops are procuring firewood. When there are columns of dust moving about in the air, it is a sign that opposition troops are getting ready to camp out.

Even seemingly insignificant signs should not be overlooked in battle. Identify the cause and analyze the situation of the enemy.

Diplomatic Negotiations

When your adversaries speak deferentially, it is a sign that they are readying themselves for invasion while gradually building up strong defense.

When your adversaries speak aggressively and display their intention to invade, it is a sign that they are preparing to retreat.

When your adversaries seek reconciliation even though they are still strong, it is a sign that they are scheming against you.

During diplomatic negotiations, calmly see through other people's intentions and deal with them resolutely.

Evaluating the Internal Affairs of the Enemy

When tanks are occupying the front position and protecting both sides of the army, it is a sign that enemy troops are positioning themselves for a battle. When adversaries are moving hurriedly, it is a sign that they are readying for the final battle. When the opposition advances and retreats, or retreats and advances, it is a sign that they are trying to provoke you to action. When opponents can barely walk with the help of a cane, it is a sign that they are weak from food shortages and resulting hunger. While on a mission to procure water, if enemy soldiers begin drinking water before they start to transport it, it is a sign that they are weak from water shortages and resulting thirst. When adversaries do not advance under obviously favorable circumstances, it is a sign that they are exhausted.

When birds are hovering over the enemy encampment, it is a sign that they have left. When soldiers are yelling at each other at night, it is a sign that they are gripped by fear. When banners are fluttering excessively, it is a sign that there is internal turmoil. When senior officers are yelling at their subordinates for no apparent reason, it is a sign that troops are fatigued from fighting and their morale is sagging. When soldiers consume valuable military horses as food, it is a sign that they are exhausting their food supply. When soldiers are putting away or discarding cooking utensils, or are being assembled in order without returning to the campsite, it is a sign that they are being forced to prepare for the final battle.

When a commander talks at length to his subordinates or is too friendly with them, it is a sign that he has lost the trust of his subordinates. When awards, prizes, and medals are handed out excessively, it is a sign that leaders are in dire straits. When punishment is administered excessively, it is a sign that the nation is in predicament. When a superior yells furiously at his subordinates and tries to please them immediately afterward, it is a sign that he is revealing his flaws because of emotional instability.

When adversaries go out of their way to dispatch military messengers and pay their respects to you, it is a sigh that they are attempting to buy time to restructure their military strength.

When the opposition is advancing with momentum without the intention to fight or leave, it is a sign that they are scheming against you. You should carefully investigate the true intentions of the enemy.

Yu-kan *(Bravery)*

Size of Troops and Military Discipline
Only those trusted by people are capable of great achievements.

The size of troops does not really matter; what matters is solidarity.

Know the status of the enemy and concentrate your military resources. Do not rush recklessly.

Do not underestimate your opponents.

Punishment should be administered with caution. However, when necessary, punishment should be administered without hesitation.

When dealing with inexperienced soldiers, punishing small mistakes will foster the feeling of defiance. It is difficult to use people who are defiant. On the other hand, when mistakes go unpunished, there will be no discipline among soldiers. It is difficult to use people who are not disciplined. Soldiers must be trained with affection.

Discipline is important in controlling the armed forces. If military discipline is strictly enforced on a daily basis, troops will be willing to obey orders. Lack of discipline will result in disobedience. Rigorous enforcement of military discipline will earn the trust of soldiers.

Terrain

There are some terrains you should not pass through or fight in.

Favorable and Unfavorable Terrain

If both camps are advancing, when you reach an area that can be accessed from four directions, positioning yourself on high ground facing south and securing a supply route will give you an edge over the enemy.

In an area that can easily be accessed but is difficult to retreat for both sides, attack the enemy only when their defense is weak. If their defense is strong, avoid attacking them; otherwise, you will struggle because of the difficult terrain.

In an area that is disadvantageous for both camps to march into, you should not respond to provocation by the enemy. Withdraw and launch a counterattack to lure them into the area.

In a small area with a narrow entrance, if you arrive there first, you should protect the entrance and await enemy troops. If the opposition arrives there first, do not engage with them. However, if the entrance is not adequately protected, devise a scheme to attack the enemy.

In rugged terrain, your troops should be situated on high ground facing south if you arrive there first. If the other side arrives there first, abandon the plan to counterattack and retreat.

When you are away from your home country, do not engage with the enemy if both camps have comparable military strength. You will be at a disadvantage.

The Road to Defeat

When you have to fight with an enemy who is ten times as powerful as your troops.

When the soldiers are strong but military officers are weak.

When military officers are strong but the soldiers are weak. When a deputy commander fights as he wishes without following orders, because he is dissatisfied with his superior's failure to recognize his ability. When a commander is faint-hearted and lacks sternness his policies are unclear and his subordinates tend to panic. Such a leader cannot deploy troops strategically.

When a commander is uninformed about the enemy's condition. Such a commander may decide to fight even though his troops are outnumbered or outclassed by the other side. He may engage with the opposition without elite units that form the core of the military.

The above conditions will lead to defeat. If a nation lacks solidarity, troops should not be mobilized. A decisive battle cannot be fought without national cohesion.

Terrain That Can be Helpful
Some terrain can be helpful in winning a battle.

It is a commander's duty to formulate plans according to the enemy's movement and terrain. A leader fighting with this knowledge will win; a leader without this knowledge will lose.

When prospects of winning are good, the commander should fight even if the sovereign is against it. When prospects of winning are poor, the commander should not fight even if the sovereign orders him to do so.

When the outcome of a battle is clear, the commander should not take credit for success; but he should take responsibility for defeat.

The commander's duty is to defend national security and the monarch's interests. Such a commander is a national treasure.

The commander should treat his subordinates as if they were his offspring. If treated in such a way, his subordinates will always accompany him, even to the bottom of a deep ravine. The commander should treat his subordinates as if they were his children. If treated in such a way, his subordinates will be happy to share their fate with him.

If subordinates are treated too kindly, they may behave disobediently. Likewise, if subordinates are treated too leniently, they may ignore orders. In such a case, it may be difficult to impose punishment even if they disregard military discipline. It is as if you were raising a spoiled brat; such a brat would prove useless for military purposes.

Probability of winning or losing

The probability of winning will be 50-50 if you are unaware of the strength of your troops or the powerfulness of enemy forces.

The probability of winning will be 50-50 if you are aware that the military power of the opposition is not overwhelming, but unaware of the true strength of your troops.

The probability of winning will be 50-50 if you are aware of the true strength of your troops and enemy forces, but uniformed about unfavorable geographical conditions.

Since skillful fighters have a full understanding of their opponents, their own troops, and geographical features, they will not waver or hesitate in their action.

Requirements for victory

Know your enemy. Know yourself.

Seize a golden opportunity.

Take advantage of favorable location and terrain.

Kyo-iku (Education)   **Sa-gyo** (Work)

Kyu-chi (Nine Types of Land)

The key to implementing a strategy is to fight when things are favorable, and not fight when things are unfavorable. When on the offensive, catch the opposition by surprise. A crucial breakthrough can happen if the entire troops make concerted efforts to fight. In order to mobilize your troops in such a way, soldiers must be placed in a dire predicament. Such ruthlessness may be required of a commander.

Adapting your tactics to the battlefield
Tactics must be adapted to the particular location where fighting will take place.

1. When fighting in your home country; unite the minds of soldiers to promote solidarity. You should avoid fighting in your home country as much as possible.
2. When you shallowly penetrated the enemy territory, do not linger there. Advance swiftly while facilitating communication among military units.
3. When the other side manages to seize a location that is advantageous to both camps, give up the idea of attacking, and quickly position your troops behind the enemy.
4. In an area that can be accessed by both sides, military units must communicate frequently with each other. Exercise caution and strengthen your defense.
5. In a border region adjacent to foreign countries, there are some areas that will earn you a good reputation once they are captured. In such areas, focus your attention on diplomatic negotiations rather than actual fighting. Form alliances with surrounding nations.
6. When you are deep in the hostile territory and have to fight being surrounded by the enemy, make sure to procure food and other goods locally.

7. When marching through forested, fortified, or swampy areas, pass through the areas swiftly because such areas make it difficult to defend yourself.

8. In an area with a narrow passage and entrance, which would require a lengthy detour when retreating, such a location allows small military units to overwhelm large ones. Devise ingenious schemes to take advantage.

9. In an area where valor is required for survival, explain to the entire troops that no other options are available than to fight. To prepare soldiers to fight desperately, deprive them of escape routes.

Forestalling Your Enemy

Good fighters in the past were skilled at throwing their opponents into confusion.

Skillful warriors prevented the front and rear units of the enemy from making concerted efforts. They drove in a wedge between the main and support units, and superiors and subordinates, to keep them from joining forces.

Expert fighters were able to exercise good judgment. They fought when prospects were good; they did not fight when prospects were poor.

When an enemy fully prepared to fight took the offensive, masterful warriors forestalled them by attacking their weak points, controlling them at will.

Good fighters carried out military operations swiftly. Expert warriors caught their adversaries off guard. They made unexpected moves by taking unconventional paths. Skilled fighters exploited the weaknesses of the enemy during negotiations to achieve their objectives.

Fighting in Enemy Territory

1. When you have penetrated deep into the hostile territory, soldiers will act in solidarity, making it difficult for the opposition to counter.

Soldiers should procure food locally. Make sure to secure sufficient food for the entire troops. Soldiers should take good rest to preserve their strength and restore their energy.

Devise surprising tactics to inflict maximum damage.

2. In the enemy territory where there is no escape route, soldiers have no choice but to fight for their life. Soldiers will become fearless when driven into a corner.

    Soldiers will keep each other in check and fight desperately without being ordered to do so. Their minds will be united without the help of disciplinary measures. They will not betray the trust of their superiors.

    To promote cohesion, forbid soldiers from spreading rumors, and keep them from harboring doubt. If this is done, soldiers will be willing to sacrifice their lives.

    It is natural that even a soldier wants to hold on to his assets and his life. When he leaves for the battleground, he may shed tears knowing that he might not come home alive. Since ancient times, it is when soldiers find themselves in dire predicaments that they render distinguished service like samurai.

Snakes of Jozan

Good warriors need to be as agile as snakes of *Jozan*. When you strike a snake in the head, its tail will attack you. When you strike a snake in the tail, its head will attack you. When you strike a snake in the trunk, its head and tail will attack you. It is possible to mobilize your troops like snakes of *Jozan*.

Skilled fighters can mobilize the entire troops at will as if they were dealing with a single person by impelling them to act in unison.

Go and Etsu used to be enemies. When people from Go and those from Etsu happened to be in the same boat, they were struck by a storm and the boat was in enormous danger. People from the two countries worked together to sail through the storm. However, in this case, mutual cooperation was not enough. The situation required political leadership. To unlock the full potential of brave men as well as weak men, natural advantages may be needed.

This strategy is used to weather a domestic crisis arising from the collapse of domestic policies. The purpose is to divert public attention away from internal affairs and refocus it on foreign affairs in order to heighten a sense of crisis. When faced with a crisis, people will have to come together by overcoming the existing conflict of interest.

Deployment to Perilous Places

To make soldiers fight in desperation, deploy them to dangerous zones.

To lead armed forces, act calmly and with dignity.

Soldiers should not be informed of military operations, plans, strategy, changes, movement, or selection of routes. Do not inform them of the objectives of these actions. Once soldiers are entrusted with tasks, have them go upstairs, and remove the ladder to cut off their escape route.

Once you have successfully marched deep into enemy territory, advance rapidly like arrows that have been released from a bowstring. Burn ships and destroy cooking pots to dash soldiers' hopes of returning alive. Do not let soldiers know where they are headed for. It is a commander's duty to drive soldiers into a corner or make them fight to the death.

The commander must assess the nature and character of a battlefield to carefully consider different fighting tactics, courses of action, and human emotion.

Foreign policies cannot be formulated without the ability to anticipate the first move of other nations. It is impossible to take advantage of favorable topography without a guide.

If any of the above items is missing, the military will not be able to prevail.

If fully-equipped troops launch an attack, the other side will not have enough time to mobilize its troops. The simple act of assuming a threatening posture can effectively isolate the enemy diplomatically. This way, you will not need to work arduously to build diplomatic relations or enlist the support of allies. You can overwhelm the enemy at will, capture their castle, and defeat their nation.

To win the hearts and minds of soldiers, provide them with unexpected monetary rewards, and, if necessary, give them special orders. By doing so, you can mobilize the entire armed forces as if they were one person.

When assigning tasks to soldiers, you do not have to explain the nature of their missions. Let them know the favorable aspects of their tasks and withhold the unfavorable aspects.

Soldiers will make frantic efforts when exposed to grave danger. Send your troops into dangerous spots.

To fight is to employ tactics. Manipulate your opponents and seize any opportunity. Concentrate your resources and catch the other side off guard. The effective use of such tactics enables you to deceive the enemy commander even after you have deployed your troops to remote regions. This is the key to becoming a good warrior.

When a War Begins

Disallow the passage of people by closing checkpoints. Ban the travel of messengers.

Convene a military meeting to establish policies and figure out the enemy's move. Act clandestinely to strike the opposition at their most vulnerable points. Engage in battle according to plans. Launch a preemptive strike to see how the other side will respond.

Initially, behave like a virgin and throw the enemy off guard.

Then, carry out an intensive attack against the enemy as swiftly as a rabbit.

The secret of success is to act meekly on the surface while at the same time drawing on your experience to resort to a variety of techniques and trickery.

Fire Attack

A capable commander should always exercise caution. He should not act hastily until preparations are made to ensure victory.

In a battle, fire and water attacks should be carried out depending on circumstances. It is important to remember that even if the enemy is defeated and their castle is captured, the outcome is a failure if the objective of the war is not achieved.

A leader should refrain from acting emotionally, and exercise good judgment when taking action. Action based on anger will ruin a nation.

Basic Rules of a Fire Attack.
A fire attack has five objectives: To inflict damage on people and horses by burning them; to cause a shortage of goods by burning military supplies; to stop the supply of *shacho* (cars) by burning; to make it difficult to store goods by burning storage facilities; to create chaos by burning campsites.

Have ignition equipment ready before launching a fire attack. Carry it out when air is dry. Choose a moment when the moon overlaps with constellations called *ki, heki, yoku,* or *shin.* That is when the wind is sure to blow.

When a fire breaks out in the enemy camp, take the offensive in concert with the outside forces. If the enemy camp is motionless even after the fire has started, do not make any move. Decide whether to advance or not after the fire spreads.

Use a spy to launch a fire attack. Start a fire inside the enemy camp. If conditions are not right for such an attack, you can start the fire from outside. A fire should be started from the upwind direction, and take the offense from the same direction. Keep in mind that the wind blowing during the day tends to persist, whereas the wind blowing at night tends to stop quickly.

The purpose of fire attack is to throw the enemy camp into confusion. A fire attack alone cannot decide the outcome of a battle. Make sure to come up with follow-up tactics. A fire attack is as effective as a water attack. However, a water attack can only cut off the water supply to the enemy, leaving their military goods intact.

Emotion and behavior

The sovereign should not take military action out of anger. Anger can be transformed into joy over time, but everything comes to an end with the demise of a nation.

A dead person will never come back to life. This is why the sovereign must act cautiously. By doing so, national security is ensured and military power is fully utilized.

Yokan (Espionage)

Kan means spy. Espionage requires secrecy. Do not let the other side know what your intentions are. Otherwise, the effectiveness of such activities will be diminished by half.

No expense should be spared to collect intelligence. Recruit competent people for this purpose and give them preferential treatment. Otherwise, it will be difficult to secure victory.

A competent leader or commander always wins because he gathers intelligence on the enemy before the enemy does. He does not rely on the power of God, his experience, or astrology to collect information. Rather, he uses spies to gather intelligence. He never underestimates the importance of espionage.

When massive troops go on an expedition, the cost of war per day will be a heavy burden on the nation and its people. Ordinary people may be drafted into the military like cows or horses. Farmers will be forced to give up farming. A war may last for several years, but its final outcome can be determined in a single day. It is foolish to neglect to collect information on the enemy because of your unwillingness to recruit and pay for spies. Such a foolish act calls your qualification as a commander and your responsibility as an adviser to the monarch into question.

Five Types of Espionage

There are five types of espionage.

1. Collecting intelligence with the help of people of the enemy country.
2. Gathering information by bribing officials of the enemy nation.
3. Coaxing spies of the adversary nation into becoming your spies.

4. Infiltrating into the enemy nation with willingness to sacrifice one's life in order to spread disinformation.

5. Returning from the adversary country to bring valuable information. Shin Huang Ti is known for being the first emperor to unify China. No other country placed more emphasis on espionage than the Qin dynasty.

Selecting and Handling Spies

Choose the most trustworthy people in the entire armed forces to act as spies. Such people deserve the most preferential treatment.

Espionage activities must be kept confidential. Those in charge of using spies need to have wisdom and good character. Otherwise, they cannot use spies effectively. Those in charge of using spies should be meticulous. Spies must be able to serve military purposes. Spies must not divulge any information, even something trivial. Espionage should not be taken lightly.

When a spy divulges secret information, he, as well as the recipient of the information, must be eliminated.

When Launching an Attack on the Enemy

Be well-informed about the enemy. Find out the identity of people ranging from the commander of garrison troops and members of his inner circle to gatekeepers, attendants, and retainers. Instruct spies to keep an eye on their movements.

When enemy spies infiltrate into your country, locate them and bribe them to win them over to your side. You should consider using them as double agents.

Gather information with the support from people of the adversary nation. Collect intelligence by bribing officials of the adversary country. Spread disinformation.

Make sure your spies in the enemy country return safely with valuable information. Double spies must be given preferential treatment.

A capable leader or commander achieves great success by selecting ingenuous people to serve as spies. Recruitment of spies is one of the most important and challenging aspects of military strategy. It forms the core of military activity.

When the Zhou dynasty (1100 BC-770 BC) conquered the Yin dynasty (1600 BC-1100 BC) to bring the whole nation under its rule, an accomplished commander with intimate knowledge of the Yin dynasty was appointed as prime minister. He proceeded to make great achievements.

BOOK TWO

The Tactics of Shokatsu Komei: Theories of Leadership

Shokatsu Komei (181-234 BC)

Shokatsu Komei was born in Yo-to, Roya-gun. His real name was Ryo. His posthumous name was Chubu (or Buko).

Komei's book of *Heiho* is a thorough overview of classical military tactics. The first part consists of theories about leadership, management, and military leaders. The second part mainly discusses Sun Tzu, capturing the essence of seven texts including *Riku-to, Shiba-ho, Utsu-ryo-shi, Riei-komon-tai, San-ryaku, The Art of War* by Sun Tzu, and *Goshi's Art of War*. Komei's book of *Heiho* contains 50 chapters. This section will attempt to convey the gist of Komei's work.

His friend, Josho, recommended Komei to Ryubi, a warlord. Ryubi ordered Josho to bring Komei to his place. Upon hearing this, Josho explained to him, "Komei is like a dragon lurking underground. Lord, if you would like to meet a person like him, you must pay him a visit."

Ryubi visited Komei three times and managed to meet Komei at the third visit. Ryubi was 47 and Komei was 27 at the time.

Judging People's Personality

It is hard to judge people. It is not always the case that a virtuous person appears virtuous and a wicked person appears wicked.

People who act politely on the surface may be disdainful of others. People who look amiable may be trying to deceive others. People who speak aggressively to others may actually be fearful. People who appear to be working hard may be concealing their selfish motives.

Seven points to consider when judging a person:

1. Ask the person to judge what is right and wrong, and take notice of his intentions.
2. Drive the person to a corner in an argument, and observe how his attitude changes.
3. Ask the person's opinion about strategy to gauge the level of his knowledge.
4. Let the person handle a difficult situation to see how courageous he is.
5. Make the person drunk, and observe his true character.
6. Offer the person a chance to serve his own interests to measure the degree of his integrity.
7. Give the person a task to determine how reliable he is. See if he can carry out the task as ordered.

Military Leaders' Capability

Each leader's capability varies considerably.

1. A leader capable of managing 10 people has the ability to identify disingenuous people and foresee dangers. Is good at controlling his subordinates.

2. A leader capable of managing 100 people works hard to fulfill his military duties from early in the morning until late at night. Is cautious when speaking.

3. A leader capable of managing 1,000 people is very thoughtful and brave. Is eager to fight in battle. Has an aversion to dishonesty.

4. A leader capable of managing 10,000 people has plenty of fight in him. Is considerate toward his subordinates and soldiers, and willing to go through unpleasant experiences with them such as hunger and coldness. Has a powerful appearance.

5. A leader capable of managing 100,000 people recruits talented people. Is loyal and tolerant. Remains unruffled even in time of disorder. Never neglects to cultivate his mind.

6. A leader capable of managing the whole nation is revered by the whole nation. Treats his people with benevolence. Earns the respect of neighboring countries with his steadfastness. Is well informed about astronomy, geography, and personnel.

Nine types of leaders

1. *Jin-sho* (benevolent leader) treats his subordinates with kindness and respect. Is willing to undergo unpleasant experiences with his subordinates such as hunger and coldness.

2. *Gi-sho* (honorable leader) responsibly fulfills his duties as a leader. Refuses to stay alive and be subjected to humiliation. Is not afraid to die to defend the honor of his country without any regard for his own interest.

3. *Rei-sho* (unpretentious leader) is principled and willing to endure hardship if necessary. Is not boastful of his high social position. Remains humble even after defeating the enemy. Is sensible and modest.

4. *Chi-sho* (wise leader) is a shrewd strategist. Manages to win a battle under unfavorable circumstances. Has the ability to turn disadvantages into advantages. Can respond to any situation.

5. *Shin-sho* (trustworthy leader) administers punishment in a fair manner regardless of a person's social standing. Is quick to give an award to someone worthy of a prize. Is strict about rewarding and punishing his subordinates.

6. *Ho-sho* (leader of the infantry) is very eager to fight. Is skilled in swordplay. Fiercely defends the borders of his country. Can run faster than a war horse.

7. *Ki-sho* (leader of the cavalry) can shoot arrows accurately while riding a horse. Leads the army when advancing and brings up the rear when retreating. Does not hesitate to climb a high mountain or go through rugged terrain.

8. *Mo-sho* (fierce leader) boosts the morale of the entire army by spearheading an attack. The more formidable the enemy, the more combative he becomes. Never recoils even when faced with powerful opponents.

9. *Tai-sho* (main leader) is tolerant, principled, and valiant. Is full of ingenuity. Treats wise people deferentially. Is willing to accept criticism.

Things Leaders Must Avoid

A leader should not be boastful of his ability. Conceit will be visible in one's attitude in the form of disrespectfulness. Disrespectfulness will lose the support of the public as well as the admiration of one's subordinates.

A leader should not be unwilling to reward his soldiers. Otherwise, soldiers will be reluctant to sacrifice their lives, and the objectives of military action will not be achieved. One's territory will become prone to invasion.

Eight qualities leaders must not have
1. An avaricious person with insatiable desire.
2. A person who is envious of talented people.
3. A person who accepts criticism as well as flattery.
4. A person who is knowledgeable about the enemy but not about himself.
5. A hesitant and indecisive person.
6. A drunkard.
7. A cowardly person who resorts to trickery.
8. A person who is all talk and no action. An insincere person.

Seven qualities of poor leaders
1. A person who is not canny—unable to make sound judgment.
2. A disrespectful person—unable to recruit talented people.
3. A person lacking in political acumen—unable to properly enforce the law.
4. A person who is disinclined to help the poor—lacks the political will even when financial resources are available.

5. An unwise person—unable to prepare for the unex
   pected.
6. An inconsiderate person—unable to prevent confiden
   tial matters from leaking.
7. A successful person who does not put in a good word fo
   his old friends—will come under public criticism whe
   defeated.

Five Qualities Required of Leaders

1. A dignified person—able to raise the morale of his subordinates.
2. A dutiful person—able to earn a good reputation.
3. A loyal person—able to form close friendships.
4. A thoughtful person—able to act generously.
5. A fully committed person—able to render distinguished service.

Five duties of leaders

1. To be familiar with the enemy's current status.
2. To make a right decision about one's course of action.
3. To know the nation's limitations.
4. To know the correct time and have a good grasp of one's subordinates.
5. To thoroughly examine the region's terrain beforehand.

Saku-sen (*Tactics*)

What Leaders Should Do

If you underestimate a wise man, you will not be able to win his heart. If you underestimate an ordinary person, you will not be able to win his full support.

What defines a leader
  A leader must win the hearts and minds of soldiers.
  A leader must administer reward and punishment in a strict manner.
  A leader must excel academically as well as athletically.
  A leader must learn to be both unyielding and flexible.
  A leader must be well versed in etiquette, music, poetry, and literature.
  A leader must prioritize love and justice over knowledge and valor.

Commanding soldiers
  When at rest, the army must lie low like fish lurking under a rock.
  When on the move, the army must attack the enemy swiftly like a river otter.
  Use flags to display your power. Use golden drums and gongs to give signals. Capture and annihilate the enemy forces.
  When retreating, soldiers must move in an orderly manner like a mountain range. Do not let your guard down.
  When advancing, soldiers must move as swiftly as a gale.
  When engaged in armed combat, soldiers must act like a ferocious tiger.
  When confronted with powerful enemies, you must resort to deception if necessary.
  When you come under all-out attack, throw the enemy

troops off their guards by retreating and lying low. Make them believe they are winning and lure them into action. Crush them by confusing them.

When the enemy forces demonstrate solidarity, drive a wedge among them.

When the enemy is strong, weaken their strength.

When chasing the fleeing enemy, soldiers must move as quickly as thunder.

Treating your soldiers

Always show deep concern for your troops.

Reassure those under attack that reinforcements are on the way.

Raise the spirits of those who are nervous.

Skillfully keep those who may rebel against you under control.

If a person insists he is falsely accused, give him an opportunity to prove his innocence.

Keep a tight rein on those who are too zealous.

Urge cowardly soldiers to pluck up their courage.

Appoint those who excel in devising strategy as close advisors.

Expel those who slander others.

Provide sufficient financial compensation for those in need.

Even when your opponents are weak, do not attack in an overbearing way.

Even when your armed forces are powerful, do not underestimate the enemy.

Do not flaunt your talent and throw your weight around.

Do not act arrogantly, just because you have won the ruler's favor.

Be sure to develop a foolproof strategy before mobilizing your troops. Launch a military operation when victory is clearly in sight.

Even when the enemy's resources, women, and children are captured, do not attempt to keep them to yourself.

If a leader treats his subordinates as recommended above, they will be eager to go to the battlefield and fight bravely.

15 Things Leaders Should Do

When taking military action, leaders must keep the following 15 things in mind. Underestimating the enemy's strength can lead to defeat.

1. Engage in espionage.
2. Be familiar with the enemy's situation.
3. Do not be intimidated by powerful enemies.
4. Do not be motivated by self-interest.
5. Administer reward and punishment evenhandedly.
6. Be able to endure humiliation.
7. Be magnanimous.
8. Do not lie.
9. Recruit new people.
10. Do not listen to slanderous remarks.
11. Take good care of soldiers.
12. Act modestly.
13. Be fully committed to serving your country.
14. Be aware of your limitations.
15. Know yourself; know your enemy.

A Good Leader

Good leaders in the past adhered to the following four principles when working with their subordinates.

1. A good leader gave adequate instructions to his troops when advancing and retreating, making sure that no one disobeyed his orders.
2. A good leader acted ethically by being respectful. He instructed his men to act in accordance with moral standards.

3. A good leader adopted an ability-based recruitment system and motivated people to work hard.
4. A good leader let it be known that he spoke truthfully and strictly administered reward and punishment.

A Mediocre Leader

A mediocre leader is the opposite of a good leader.

When advancing, a mediocre leader proceeds recklessly, creating havoc. When retreating, a mediocre leader is unable to keep his troops together, leading to a total collapse.

A mediocre leader arbitrarily administers reward and punishment. His subordinates grow distrustful of him. A mediocre leader is overly enthusiastic and incapable of exercising restraint. A mediocre leader dismisses talented people and appoints flatterers to important positions. A mediocre leader will inevitably lose a battle.

A Commander's Authority

A commander determines the fate of soldiers under his command and the key to the outcome of the battle. The fate of the country is in a commander's hands.

By the time a commander leads the army into battle, a military strategy has already been developed. This strategy serves as basic guidance for the army; however, military action must constantly be adapted to changing situations.

A commander should be given absolute discretion. A commander's right to exercise control freely must be guaranteed. This will prevent men under his command from pursing their own interests and losing their motivation for fighting gallantly. If the right to exercise control is not guaranteed, even a sagacious, valiant commander will not be able to protect his own life.

Occasionally a commander may ignore the ruler's orders. The ruler must relegate the authority to administer reward and punishment to the commander on the battlefield.

Commander's Attitudes Toward his Subordinates

Strictness and thoughtfulness are both important. A good commander in the past treated his subordinates as if they were his own children.

When faced with obstacles, a good commander took the initiative in overcoming the difficulties.

A good commander gave his subordinates credit for military accomplishments. He took good care of the injured and held memorial services for the fallen soldiers. A good commander shared his food with the hungry. He took off his clothes and gave them to those who were chilled to the bone. When hiring wise men, a good commander treated them with utmost respect. He rewarded courageous men for their distinguished service.

A Commander's Leadership

Once, when a nation was in a predicament, the king appointed a competent man as commander. On the day of the appointment, the king gave the new commander an ax, a symbol of military power, and said the following: "As a commander, you will be in charge of the army. You must catch the enemy off guard. Do not make a futile attempt to confront powerful opponents. Do not look down on your subordinates just because you are a commander. Listen to the voices of your subordinates. Do not forget your duties in a rush to achieve success. Work alongside your subordinates under any circumstances, in cold weather, hot weather, difficult times, and peaceful times. By doing so, your subordinates will make frantic efforts to win the battle." Then, the king went to the northern gate to see the new commander off and said, "Deciding the course of action all depends on timing. Your orders are absolute in the military. You may ignore the king's orders."

Delegating complete authority to the commander makes his position unshakable, enabling him to use his men as he wishes. It will enable him to win a battle and his triumph will be widely known. His legacy will be handed down to posterity.

Incompetent Commanders

A fearless commander who trivializes the importance of human life may be manipulated into bringing about his own self-destruction.

An impatient, short-tempered commander may become restless if forced to wait.

An avaricious commander intent on enriching himself may be tempted to engage in clandestine communication if he stands to benefit from it.

An excessively compassionate commander who is too lenient may become exhausted when placed under psychological pressure.

A wise, but indecisive commander may find himself in a difficult position when he comes under all-out attack.

A calculating commander lacking in the ability to take action may prove incompetent when forced to bring a swift end to a battle.

What Commanders Should Do on the Battlefield

Don't complain of thirst before obtaining water from a well. Don't complain of hunger before preparing meals. Don't complain of fatigue before drawing curtains. Don't complain of coldness before lighting a bonfire.

A commander should spend time with his soldiers without using a fan on hot days or resting in a shelter on rainy days.

Staff Officers

The armed forces include staff officers who assist commanding officers in examining the advantages and disadvantages of military operations. Staff officers consist of high, middle, and low ranking officers.

High-ranking officers – People who are admired by everyone should be appointed as high-ranking officers. Such a person must be an eloquent speaker who is highly ingenious and creative. He must also be very knowledgeable and versatile.

Middle-ranking officers – People who are as powerful as a tiger or bear, as agile as a monkey, and as strong as steel should be appointed as middle-ranking officers. A man with a brilliant mind like a good sword should be recruited for this position.

Low-ranking officers – A talkative person who sometimes makes sensible comments is a mediocre serviceman with no notable skill or talent. Such a person should be chosen as a low-ranking officer.

The Responsibilities of Armed Forces

Weapons are designed to kill; however, excessive reliance on weapons may result in failure. A commander's job is not easy. If he is not cautious in dealing with things, he may bring about his own destruction.

A good commander in charge of the strongest army does not depend on the might of the army alone. A good commander who enjoys the full confidence of the monarch does not take advantage of his power.

A good soldier will not lose his fighting spirit even when humiliated by his enemies. A good soldier always passes up an opportunity to serve his self-interest. A good soldier always puts national interests first. He will never be tempted by beautiful women or delicious food and drink.

Formation of Military Units

It is of the utmost importance to form military units based on the ability of each soldier.

Hokoku-tai (patriot regiment) – Choose someone who loves to fight more than anything else and enjoys being on the battlefield, someone who can maintain his composure even when confronted by the most powerful enemy.

Totsugeki-tai (attack regiment) – Select someone who is enthusiastic, athletic, and quick to act.

Tokko-tai (special regiment) – Choose someone with good legs who can run faster than a horse.

Kishu-tai (surprise attack regiment) – Pick someone who can skillfully shoot arrows while riding a horse and hit the target one hundred percent of the time.

Shageki-tai (shooting regiment) – Select a skilled archer who can bring down an enemy combatant at the first attempt without missing the target.

Hogeki-tai (artillery regiment) – Choose someone who is strong enough to fully draw a stone bow and hit a distant target without fail. Always make sure to put the right person in the right place depending on each soldier's ability when forming military units.

Forewarned is Forearmed

A nation should never neglect its national defense. Do not neglect national defense because any error in national defense may have irreversible consequences. The nation may suffer crushing defeat against the enemy, resulting in foreign domination of its land.

Only highly capable people can serve as commanders. When faced with difficulties, the monarch must consult with his men without taking the time to eat or sleep and choose a competent person to be a commander.

A commander must be able to have soldiers obey his orders and act in an orderly manner. He should not overwork his subordinates. A commander should not be motivated by self-interest. When soldiers are suffering from hunger or cold weather, he should feel sympathy for them and try to alleviate their suffering.

A commander should not allow soldiers to say something superstitious or fanatical. A commander should not allow soldiers to engage in disorderly conduct, which can confuse the judgment of senior officers.

Soldiers should not be allowed to ignore orders of their superiors out of youthful hastiness or act arbitrarily based on their own judgment.

No one should be allowed to misappropriate military funds and enrich himself.

Orders and Tools

When giving signals, produce clear sounds that stimulate the ear.

Flags and banners must have conspicuous colors that stimulate the eye. Such flags and banners are useful tools to have soldiers obey orders.

Punishment should be meted out in a strict manner. Bans and punishments are useful tools to stimulate the mind, thereby ensuring that soldiers follow orders. Make sure to properly enforce the above recommendations. These are tools to control soldiers at will and encourage them to advance without fear of death.

Understanding the Source of Power

When you attack the evil forces by riding the tide of time, enormous power will be unleashed, even surpassing the power of saints.

When you join forces to claim victory, great achievements will be made, even surpassing the greatness of virtuous rulers.

When you realize your full potential by knowing the source of your power, you will triumph over any formidable adversary you may encounter.

Three Conditions That Can Work to Your Advantage

To win a battle, make sure that conditions are favorable.

Ten no toki (heavenly moment) – This is a time when the sun, the moon, and five stars appear in the sky with no ominous comets, and wind and energy are in harmony.

Chi no sei (advantageous terrain) – This is an inhospitable terrain that keeps enemy forces away, including areas surrounded by precipitous cliffs or protected by vast rivers and ocean.

Hito no ri (prudent people) – This is a situation where both the monarch and commanders are prudent, soldiers are well disciplined and obey orders, and there is ample food. This is a state in which the nation is protected by impenetrable fortification.

By being aware of the three conditions, you can turn the tide in your favor. The understanding of *ten no toki* and *chi no sei* requires sound judgment on the part of commanders. *Hito no ri* can be achieved through commanders' efforts.

Taking Advantage of Topography
Military tactics must be adapted to specific terrain.

- Terrain suitable for the infantry – forested mountains, hilly land, plateaus, dry riverbeds.
- Terrain suitable for the cavalry – foothills of mountains that are densely covered with vines.
- Terrain suitable for fighting with stone bows – areas near forested gorges with mountains in the background.
- Terrain suitable for fighting with long spears – flatlands with sparse grass which allow soldiers to move freely.
- Terrain suitable for fighting with pikes – wetlands interspersed with reeds and bamboos.

Adapting Military Strategy to Terrain
Fighting in the woods – Raise banners by day and beat golden drums by night. Swords should be used as weapons. Set up an ambush and launch a frontal attack on the enemy while confusing them by attacking from behind.

Fighting on the grassland – Before launching an attack, examine the roads. Set up a military camp every 25 miles (40 km) and a watchtower with a banner every 12 miles (20 km), making them stand together along the roads. Lift the morale of troops by beating golden drums wildly. Using swords and shields as weapons, be prepared to stun the enemy forces.

Fighting in the ravine – This terrain is suitable for an ambush. Encourage troops to fight bravely to find a path to victory. First select soldiers who are good runners and position them in rocky areas. Then, dispatch a suicide squad, followed by a volley of arrows. Troops bearing swords come next, who will force the enemy to engage in hand-to-hand combat.

Fighting on the water – Use ships. Soldiers must be trained to fight on the water. Baffle the enemy by flying flags and banners in all available places. As a volley of arrows is fired, attack the enemy along the flow of the river. Strong fences should be built to protect against the enemy's counterattack. Meet the enemy's counterattack with swords.

Fighting at night – Do not let the enemy know about the details of military operations. Troops should be deployed covertly to catch the enemy off guard. If appropriate, confuse the senses of enemy soldiers by covering the battleground with torches while beating drums wildly, and finish off the enemy in one attack.

How you Command your Military Determines the Outcome of Battle

Maintain discipline among soldiers even in peaceful time. In time of war, military strength should be put into full force as is expected of the armed forces.

Troops should advance with unstoppable momentum. Even when ordered to retreat, troops should be on the lookout to thwart the enemy's move.

Military units should collaborate closely with each other. They must team up to overcome difficulties. The military as a whole must be united in its efforts, and should not be deceived by the enemy's attempts to create divisions. The morale of troops should be high, ready to repel to the enemy's fierce attack.

Observing Military Law

A commander is in charge of millions of subordinates and soldiers. If lower ranking officers dutifully obey his orders and no one dares to challenge him, this indicates that military law is strictly enforced.

A commander should maintain complete control over the military. By enforcing military law and meting out reward and punishment, his subordinates will not disobey his orders. A commander should never take military law lightly.

Failure to Observe Military Law

A road to self-destruction: a commander not granted the authority to administer reward and punishment; his subordinates are lacking in respect and courtesy. Sooner or later, such a commander will be headed for self-destruction even if he succeeds in unifying the nation and amassing a fortune.

Ten-toki-hito
(Ten: Sky; Heaven
Toki: Time
Hito: Ma)

Good and Bad Tactics

There three types of military tactics:

Worst tactics – A commander is frantically focusing on the immediate outcome. A commander himself is going into the front lines and comes under attack by arrows, resulting in high casualties on both sides with no clear signs of victory or defeat.

Acceptable tactics – Troops are positioned face to face with the enemy forces. The troops gradually close in on the enemy. Soldiers run around on horses and shoot arrows. The morale of the troops is bolstered to create fear and restlessness among the enemy soldiers.

Best Tactics – The best tactics is to win without engaging in a battle. A commander should foresee what will happen and take preemptive action. Problems must be prevented and things must not be allowed to get out of control. Action should be taken in such a way that the need to apply the penal code is eliminated.

Using Fukushin, Jimoku, Soga

Fukushin (the right hand man) – He must be highly intelligent with well rounded knowledge. Without *fukushin*, it is as if you are groping your way in the darkness, which prevents you from taking decisive action.

Jimoku (the man who works as someone's eyes and ears) – He must be cool-headed and tight-lipped. Without *jimoku*, it is as if you are sitting alone in the darkness.

Soga (the man who works as someone's arms and legs) – He must be valiant and undaunted by the enemy. Without *soga*, it is as if you are trying to eat something poisonous to satisfy extreme hunger. You may end up ruining your life.

Ten, Toki, Hito

In order to prevail, a commander must not go against *ten* (objective factors), *toki* (timing), or *hito* (human factors).

Going against *toki*—*Ten* and *hito* are right, but *toki* is wrong.

Going against *ten*—*Toki* and *hito* are right, but *ten* is wrong.

Going against *hito*—*Ten* and *toki* are right, but *hito* is wrong.

A wise man will not take military action until *ten*, *toki*, and *hito* are right.

Four things to remember

1. To fight is to make an unexpected move.
2. To devise a scheme is to keep everything strictly confidential.

3. To command the military is to use will power.
4. The hearts and minds of the entire army must be united.

Goku-i *(Secret Principle)*

Adjusting Military Tactics

Areas densely covered with vegetation are suitable for guerrilla warfare. Densely forested areas are suitable for surprise attacks. Woods at the front with no object in-between that can be used as cover are suitable for trench warfare.

When a small unit is attacking a big unit, the attack should be launched at twilight. When a big unit is attacking a small unit, the attack should be launched at dawn.

When there is an abundant supply of weapons and ammunitions, quick settlement through swift action is recommended.

When both sides are confronting each other across a river, if visibility is low due to gusty winds, a pincer movement is recommended.

What Determines the Outcome of a Battle

Secrets of success

1. Competent people are offered key positions while incompetent people are excluded.
2. Soldiers are relaxed and happy. They are pleased to obey orders from the commander.
3. Soldiers are eager to render distinguished service and all fired up.
4. The system of reward and punishment is implemented properly.

Signs of defeat

1. Soldiers neglect their military duties and become restless at trivial matters.
2. Soldiers frequently break military law. Commanders are distrustful of soldiers. Soldiers show little courtesy.
3. When soldiers are overly afraid of the enemy, they are

calculating and may be tempted to act in their own self-interest.

4. Soldiers respond emotionally to seemingly divine messages. They often talk about good or bad fortune.

When You Should Not Fight Against an Enemy Nation
1. When the nation has wise, talented people in key positions.
2. When the nation has an abundant supply of food.
3. When the nation has superior weapons and equipment.
4. When the nation enjoys good relationships with neighboring countries.
5. When the nation is backed by powerful countries.

Differences Between Success and Failure
Sages turn to heaven for guidance, sagacious men turn to nature for guidance, and wise men turn to history for guidance.

A conceited man will end up digging his own grave. An egocentric man will sow the seeds of trouble. A talkative man will break his word. A man who flaunts his talent lacks thoughtfulness.

Those who reward undeserving men will be deserted. Those who punish innocent men will be resented. Those who behave emotionally will ruin their lives.

When You Should Attack An Enemy Nation
1. When the enemy nation is exhausted from a protracted military expedition and food is scarce.
2. When citizens of the enemy nation are buckling under the high cost of a military expedition.
3. When military commands are not thoroughly carried out.
4. When weapons and construction equipment are in short supply.

5. When the enemy nation lacks consistent military strategy.
6. When the enemy nation is isolated without support.
7. When senior officers do not show concern for troops.
8. When reward and punishment are arbitrarily administered.
9. When the military as a whole lacks discipline.
10. When the enemy nation is supercilious after a victory.

Three opportunities

A good commander achieves success by never failing to take advantage of opportunities. There are three opportunities: change in circumstances, change in direction, and change in prospects.

Change in circumstances – When circumstances are favorable, it is unwise not to take advantage.

Change in direction – When things are headed in the favorable direction, it is unwise not to take advantage.

Change in prospects – When prospects are bright, it is cowardly not to take action promptly.

Comparing Military Strength

You can determine which country will win by comparing their military strength.

- Which monarch is better?
- Which country has wiser commanders?
- Which country has superior government officials?
- Which country has more food supplies?
- Which country has better-trained soldiers?
- Which military looks more imposing?
- Which country has superior military horses?
- Which country has an advantage in terms of geographical features?
- Which country is more feared by neighboring nations?
- Which country is in better financial shape?

- Which country has superior staff officers?
- Which country's citizens enjoy more stability?

Indicators of the Status of the Enemy

When both sides are confronting each other without making a move, it means that both sides are relying on strong defense. When the enemy is highly provocative, it means that it is trying to lure your troops into pushing forward.

When trees are swinging without wind, it means that soldiers and tanks are on the move. When dust is stirred up low over a wide swath of land, it means that an attack is imminent.

When the enemy messenger speaks aggressively, suggesting the possibility of forcing their way through, it means that the enemy forces are starting to withdraw.

When the enemy is neither advancing nor retreating, it means that it is vulnerable to attack. When soldiers are marching with the help of a cane, it means that they are suffering from hunger.

When enemy forces are not advancing even when conditions are favorable, it means that they are extremely exhausted. When you see a flock of birds hovering over the enemy's camping ground, it means that the enemy forces have already left.

When soldiers are talking to each other loudly at night, it means that they are gripped by fear. When troops lack discipline and commanders have no authority, it means that the soldiers are disdainful of the commanders. When you see flags fluttering, it means that a chaotic situation is developing. When senior officers vent their anger on their subordinates, it means that they are tired from a protracted military expedition.

When awards are handed out excessively, it means that the enemy is in predicament. When punishment is administered excessively, it means that the enemy is in serious trouble.

When the enemy dispatches an envoy to offer apology, it means that they are trying to give their troops some rest. When the enemy offers plenty of gifts in an attempt to curry favor, it means that they are trying to win you over to their side.

Shi-ko *(Consideration)*

A Good Loser Never Perishes

Monarchs who govern their country justly do not rely on military might. Monarchs who were called a sage strove to stabilize the life of common people. They did not depend on military forces during their lifetime. Monarchs adept at commanding the military did not take military action.

In ancient China, Shun established penal codes. Because judges were fair in their handling of cases, common people rarely attempted to deceive those in power or violated the law, leading to lasting peace.

Monarchs skillful in military tactics did not venture to engage in battle. When U conquered a tribe called Yubyo, the only thing he did was to perform a dance with Kanu, after which he returned home.

Monarchs who excelled at commanding soldiers on the battlefield did not let their country be destroyed.

Monarchs who were a good loser saved their country from ruin. Shooh of So, which was attacked by Go, fled to Shin, where he managed to secure support, and eventually returned to his country.

Flexibility is stronger than firmness

A good commander is both flexible and firm. He uses weak force to overwhelm powerful force. He uses flexibility to prevail over firmness. Weak force and flexibility alone will inevitably result in failure; powerful force and firmness alone will inevitably lead to ruin. Ideally, the middle path between flexibility and firmness should be taken.

Take the enemy by surprise

In order to respond effectively to the enemy's moves and ensure victory, you must take the enemy by surprise whenever there is an opportunity.

Harmonious relationships
Harmonious relationships are important for maintaining discipline in armed forces. When such relationships exist, soldiers will be willing to fight without being forced to do so.

Discord that Leads to Failure
1. There is antagonism among senior officers.
2. Soldiers refuse to obey orders.
3. When a good plan is formulated, but is not implemented.
4. Subordinates are critical to their superiors.
5. Name-calling and obstruction are rampant.

How to Motivate Your Subordinates
1. Guarantee handsome salaries—talented people will flock to the jobs.
2. Be respectful and keep your word—your subordinates will be willing to sacrifice their lives.
3. Grant favors to soldiers and enforce the law fairly—your subordinates will be happy to obey orders.
4. Take the initiative— your subordinates will no longer hesitate.
5. Record any good deeds, even trivial ones. Give rewards for achievements, even insignificant ones— your subordinates will be willing to work hard.
6. The purpose of management is to create an environment where people are encouraged to work and feel motivated.

Reasons for Bravery
When defense is strong, soldiers will fight bravely. Sharp weapons and heavy armor enable soldiers to fight courageously. Without such equipment, it is as if soldiers were fighting without

any clothes. If arrows do not hit their targets, it is as if no arrows were used. If arrows do not penetrate the targets deep enough, it is as if arrowheads were missing. Bees and scorpions are not afraid of their enemies because they can rely on their venomous stingers.

Lack of watchtowers is equivalent to lack of national defense.

If a commander lacks courage, it is as if there were no commander.

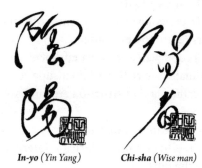

In-yo (*Yin Yang*)   **Chi-sha** (*Wise man*)

BOOK THREE

The Tactics of Shokatsu Komei: The Art of War

One's progress may come to a halt when standing at a crossroads. In order to make further progress in life, one will need to recharge intellectually and put his knowledge to good use. The book on the art of war discusses military strategy, tactics, and methods. It provides valuable insight into, and analysis of, warfare.

et-shoku (*Ironclad Rule*)

Holding Power Over the Military

The key to holding power over the military is to establish a formidable reputation that enables one to mobilize the entire armed forces freely. In order to fulfill one's duties, one must be given the authority to perform those tasks. The same can be said for any organization.

Organizational Implosion
The following 5 types of people contribute to implosion of an organization. Prompt action must be taken.

1. A person who cajoles his friends into forming a gang and slanders competent people.
2. A person who dresses ostentatiously.
3. A person who speaks as if possessed by the supernatural, often referring to sorcery, without the ability to perform such acts.
4. A person who ignores social norms and arbitrarily instigates the public.
5. A person who secretly conspires with enemies if it is in his interest to do so.

Main Military Objectives

It is important to strengthen border defense and be prepared for major unrest. To achieve such goals, peace and security of a nation must be ensured, while making sure that the nation has a high standing in the world and no atrocity is tolerated.

A Nation Must Have Military Power.
A nation with powerful military forces can enjoy peace and security. A nation with weak military forces faces risk of demise. A military commander will decide the fate of the country. If the commander is unable to fulfill his responsibilities, he is unqualified to be a leader of the people. Then, a monarch will be unable to perform his duties as a monarch, making it difficult for him to command the military.

Use knowledge to govern a country. Use force to control the military. To govern a country, gain support of foreign ethnic groups. To control the military, appease domestic feudal lords.

A quick way to rule over various groups is to resort to power or authority rather than persuasion. First, treat them with respect. Demonstrate your power when dealing with them. Resort to power only when your benevolence fails to convince them.

Military Forces can be Deadly.
Troops should be deployed only when necessary. Otherwise, use of armed forces can jeopardize a nation's survival. In a tranquil time, troops should be ready like a fully drawn bow. Dynamic mobilization of troops will make them invincible against any enemy.

A commander must not be inconsiderate. Soldiers must not let their enthusiasm wain. If a country recklessly goes to war without a sense of solidarity among troops, even one-million-strong troops will not pose a threat to the enemy. Such troops are no more than a disorderly crowd.

Secrets of Military Tactics

Keep operation plans confidential.

When attacking the enemy, move as fast as a gale. On the battlefield, strike the enemy swiftly like a torrent for quick victory.

A good strategist will not be swayed by emotion. A strategist who has devised flawless plans will not be intimidated by enemies. A wise man is someone who develops flawless plans before launching an attack to ensure victory.

A foolish man is someone who engages in battle without assessing the prospects of success and later attempts to find a way out.

A winner is someone who naturally goes with the flow and follows the right path.

A loser is someone who takes a shortcut and gets lost.

A commander must maintain his dignity. Soldiers must do everything in their power to fulfill their duties. This will enable troops to realize their true potential.

Move with the flow to gain momentum and increase destructive power.

Preparing for military action

The outcome of military action depends on prospects. Do not engage in battle without being prepared. Avoid military action when there is little prospect of success. Dispatch troops when the following conditions are met.

Essential requirements

1. Clarify the way of the universe.
2. Understand the mental tendency of people.
3. Conduct combat training repeatedly.
4. Establish a clear system of reward and punishment.
5. Analyze the enemy's military strategy and tactics.
6. Examine road conditions.
7. Distinguish safe routes from dangerous ones.
8. Analyze the military capability of both sides.
9. Be able to know when to advance or retreat.
10. Take advantage of an opportunity.
11. Reinforce defense.
12. Bolster the morale of troops.
13. Allow soldiers to realize their full potential.
14. Formulate a detailed operation plan.
15. Have soldiers be prepared to sacrifice their lives.

Formulation and Implementation of a Plan

A commander is in charge of soldier's lives and national security. A flawless plan must be formulated. Commands must be carried out smoothly. The plan must be implemented as swiftly as a hawk or falcon swooping down on its prey.

Combining *Ki* and *Sei*

The key to success is to understand changes in *ki* and *sei* and how to combine them in various ways. *Ki* – Strategy or method adapted to particular situations. Examples include taking a detour or launching a flank attack. *Sei* – General or basic strategy or method. Examples include a strategic operation carried out by the main unit.

Military Action
Place emphasis on innovative schemes and clever manipulation. Draw up a plan that combines flexibility and firmness.

Attitude—Move as swift as a rainstorm; be as calm as the ocean or mountain. Do something unexpected like yin and yang.

Move like bountiful Mother Earth, Heaven, or powerful rivers such as the Yellow River and the Yangtze River.

Carry out attacks continuously like the cycles of the sun, moon, stars, four seasons, or *go-gyo* (five elements).

Military action requires procurement of weapons and food, which may lead to inflation and suffering of the people. Utmost caution is needed.

Military expeditions may cause various problems. Strike the enemy just once. Carrying out quick attacks a few times is not recommended.

Be mindful of the limits of national wealth. Avoid making futile attempts. Ensure the peace and security of the nation by dismissing incompetent people.

Secrets of Successful Implementation of Strategy
Good offense throws the enemy's defense strategy into turmoil. Good offense does not rely on arms.

Good defense creates no opportunity for the enemy to attack.

Good defense does not rely on fortifications. Building a castle with deep moats does not necessarily translate into good defense. Troops armed with sharp weapons and heavy armor are not necessarily the best soldiers.

When the enemy's defense is reinforced, attack their weak points.

When the enemy forces start moving after clearing out the camp, take them by surprise.

When both sides are on the move, your troops should be stationed in an area with favorable geographical conditions.

When the enemy forces are lying low even after your troops have been deployed, strike them on the right and left flanks.

When your enemy is a coalition of several nations, attack the leading nation first.

Preparing for the enemy's attack in an untimely manner without considering geographical factors will weaken your troops. To minimize damage, form teams consisting of the weak and the strong, and the spineless and the brave, and move the entire troops swiftly, ensuring front-to-back and side-to-side coordination.

Know Your Enemy's Situation

To have your troops ready, you must have a firm grasp of the enemy's situation. You need to be aware of the topography and terrain, develop an operation plan, and make sure that orders are passed along the chain of command.

Provoke the enemy troops to see how they react. Put together various types of information to assess the enemy's military power. Undertake a strategic operation to find out the advantages and disadvantages of the topography of the region where enemy troops are stationed. Gather information to gauge the level of enthusiasm among enemy combatants.

Have a minor skirmish with the enemy to judge its military strength. Stay away from enemies with great military power. Catch the enemy off guard.

Twenty Things to Remember

Remember the following when taking military action.

1. If you succeed in gaining momentum, you will win.
2. A long-distance expedition will create a shortage of food
3. When troops are stationed in an arid region, they will suffer from water shortages.
4. Leakage of plans will lead to defeat.
5. Destabilization efforts by the enemy will exhaust your troops.
6. A sense of urgency will be lost when tranquility prevails
7. Doubts will be aroused when there is no fighting.
8. Self-interest will foster indecisiveness.
9. Unusually harsh punishment will create passive attitudes
10. Promise of reward will create enthusiasm.
11. When you are losing ground, you will become pessimistic.
12. When you are building up momentum, you will become confident.
13. When you are beleaguered, you will be stricken with apprehension.
14. When you take the lead, you will be overwhelmed by fear.
15. Loud talking on a moonless night will startle soldiers, creating confusion.
16. Being off track will hinder implementation of a plan.
17. You may become trapped when driven into a corner.
18. A prolonged military expedition may lead to defeat.
19. A strategic plan developed in advance will be of great help.
20. Raise banners conspicuously when issuing commands to make sure that soldiers proceed in the same direction. Beat golden drums to get attention. Use axes to unite the minds of soldiers. Encourage soldiers to render distinguished service by promising reward. Correct misbehav-

ior by imposing punishment. Use banners during the day when visibility is good. Use fire and drums to send signals at night when visibility is poor. Those who disobey orders should be disciplined with an ax.

Adapting Military Tactics to Terrain

When fighting in hilly terrain, do not launch an attack when your troops are stationed in the lowlands with enemy forces occupying the highlands.

When fighting on the water, do not launch an attack when your troops are situated downstream with enemy forces located upstream.

When fighting in the grasslands do not advance your troops into areas densely covered with vegetation.

When fighting on the flat plain, position your troops in areas that allow free movement.

When fighting on the road, be ready for individual combat, since soldiers will not be able to spread out.

Kyu-chi (Nine Land) and Kyu-hen (Nine Incidents)

Military strategy must be adapted to particular types of land.
Kyu-chi (nine land)—Battlefield situations can be categorized into nine types.

1. *San-chi*—Avoid fighting in your own territory.
2. *Kei-chi*—Keep advancing your troops after entering the enemy territory.
3. *So-chi*—If both camps are attempting to capture a site, refrain from attacking once it is taken by the enemy.
4. *Ko-chi*—Military units should maintain good communication with each other in a territory vulnerable to attack by both camps.
5. *Ku-chi*—In a territory penetrated by several nations, place emphasis on diplomatic negotiations.
6. *Ju-chi*—Once your troops have penetrated deeply into the enemy territory, things should be procured locally.
7. *Hi-chi*—Quickly pass through terrains that are difficult

to march through such as woods, mountains, and wetlands.

8.   *I-chi*—Rely on a clever scheme in a territory with a
narrow passage that makes it difficult to withdraw.

9.   *Shi-chi*—In a territory where a quick, decisive battle is
impossible, be prepared for drawn-out fighting.

Nine Incidents—Fighting Methods Suitable for Nine Types of Land

1.   Do not launch a front attack on enemy troops stationed
on high ground.

2.   Do not mount a front attack on enemy forces positioned
against the hill.

3.   Do not chase enemies who are purposely retreating.

4.   Do not fight conventionally when dealing with elite troops.

5.   Do not jump on decoys dispatched by the enemy.

6.   When enemy soldiers are longing to return home, do not
force them to engage in battle.

7.   When enemy forces come under siege, make sure to
secure an escape route. Never completely encircle the
enemy.

8.   Do not carelessly approach enemy forces that are driven
into a corner.

9.   Do not overstay in a hostile territory that is far away from
your home country. Be aware of the nine types of land
during battle. In addition to applying the nine principles
of offense, in order to prevail, you must be familiar with
the character of senior officers and military schemes.
Knowing these three things will ensure victory.

The Importance of Espionage

The military uses five types of spies. Only a commander of good
character with profound wisdom can effectively manage espionage activities.

Advantages of Using the Five Types of Spies

Troops can position themselves at a vantage point, which enables them to anticipate the arrival of enemy forces from afar. Troops can take enough rest, which allows them to wait until the enemy becomes exhausted. Troops can eat well, which allows them to wait until the enemy becomes hungry. Troops can build up their strength, which allows them to wait until the enemy becomes weak. Troops can take up strategic positions first, enabling them to wait for the enemy forces to position themselves at unfavorable locations.

Troops can be mobilized on a large scale, enabling them to wait for the enemy platoons to arrive. The morale of troops can be boosted, enabling them to wait for the enemy's spirits to dampen. Troops can stage an ambush, enabling them to be prepared for the enemy's attack.

Five Types of Spies

1. Spies that gather information from residents of the enemy nation.
2. Spies that obtain information from civil servants of the enemy nation.
3. Spies that coax the enemy's secret agents into switching allegiance.
4. Spies that infiltrate into the enemy nation, fully prepared to sacrifice their lives.
5. Spies that return home safely from the enemy nation to contribute to the prosperity of their country.

Performance Evaluation

To govern effectively, you must evaluate the performance of government employees. Retain only the best employees and discharge incompetent ones.

A wise ruler must be able to exercise sound, impartial judgment when assessing someone's ability. He should pay attention to people of lower socioeconomic status, local government employees, and ordinary people, making sure that he is not overlooking anyone in the country. This will enable him to hire truly capable workers.

People gravitate toward a wise ruler like clouds, allowing him to govern effectively. This will be possible only when performance evaluation is properly carried out.

What Kind of Civil Servants are Harmful to People?
1. A person who takes advantage of his position to enrich himself. Such a civil servant of small caliber abuses his authority and engages in misconduct. He holds on to power and seizes people's properties, giving rise to political corruption.
2. A person who arbitrarily enforces the law. Such a civil servant may severely punish petty crime while condoning grave offense. He may even punish innocent people, some of whom may be sentenced to death. He is unduly lenient with those in power while being excessively strict with the powerless, sometimes making false accusations against them.
3. A person who repeatedly engages in wrongdoing. Such a civil servant attempts to destroy evidence of his wrongdoing by silencing whistleblowers. He may even try to eliminate such informers.

4. A person who manipulates the director general to enrich himself. Such a civil servant holds real power in the shadow of the director general. He does favors for his friends while mistreating people he dislikes. He disregards the law and introduces legislation to increase taxes. He is busy lining his pockets, exploiting people like a leech.

5. A person who is obsessed with his own success. Such a civil servant is lenient in administration of punishment in an effort to earn a reputation. He intervenes in the affairs of the private sector, taking jobs away from people.

These five types of civil servants should be dismissed immediately. When recruiting staff, these types of people must be avoided. A worker's competence will be apparent in three years after hiring. Keep only competent employees and fire incompetent ones.

Reward and Punishment
Administration of reward and punishment

1. The purpose of giving rewards is to encourage distinguished service. Be fair when giving rewards. Be impartial when administering punishment. How a reward is given will determine whether a man of valor will fight to death; a wicked man will know what action is not permitted. Never give rewards to those who do not deserve it. Otherwise, those who actually serve with distinction will be disgruntled.

2. The purpose of administering punishment is to eradicate violation of law. Never punish those who are innocent. Otherwise, those who abide by law will be resentful.
    A country was lost because of a bowl of sheep soup. When the king of Chusan hosted a party, it so happened that Shibaki and his attendants did not get to eat a bowl

of soup. Shibaki, who harbored a grudge about this, fled to the nation of So and attacked Chusan, forcing the king to escape from his country. The king later lamented having lost his country because of a bowl of soup.

Like So-oh, some rulers faced risk of downfall because they were deceived into killing innocent people.

Five Mistakes That Can Jeopardize a Nation

1. A nation that turns a blind eye to those who break the law and commit crime while punishing those who are innocent. This will lead to the dissolution of troops.
2. A nation that is bursting with anger. In such a country, it is difficult to maintain law and order consistently.
3. A nation where criteria for reward and punishment are arbitrary, which discourage subordinates from rendering distinguished service.
4. A nation that constantly changes its orders, making it difficult for people to obey the law.
5. A nation where officials confuse public duty with private life. Subordinates of such officials will be double-faced.

Distinguishing Reward and Punishment—How a Commander Can Prevent Blunders

Govern in a respectable manner to prevent people from breaking the law. Be frugal and do not indulge in luxuries.

Select a loyal person to serve as judge. Choose an impartial person and give him the authority to administer reward and punishment. Clarify the system of reward and punishment so that your subordinates will be happy to obey your orders.

In a country where countless people are starving on the streets while the horses kept in the king's stables are plump, it is hardly surprising if common people start complaining that they are treated as worthless. A commander should never treat his subordinates this way.

Establish clear criteria for reward and punishment. Provide reward to those who render distinguished service based on the criteria. Punish those who violate orders given to them.

When reward and punishment are administered arbitrarily, loyal vassals may be put to death despite their innocence. On the other hand, treacherous vassals may be assigned to important posts even though they haven't rendered any distinguished service.

Reward anyone who makes a significant contribution, even those whom you find distasteful. Punish anyone who commits a crime, even those who are close to you.

The right path is to practice impartiality.

Disciplinary Action Against Those Who Disobey Orders

Violators must be disciplined. Those who take things lightly, underestimate, steal, deceive, disobey, disturb, or lead others in the wrong direction must be disciplined.

Such violations should never be condoned especially in a military setting. If left unpunished, they will surely bring disaster. A commander must discipline those who ignore orders to demonstrate the authority he has been granted.

Under the military penal code, there are different levels of discipline. A minor offense might result in a reprimand, where a major offense might require a severe penalty. All violators must be disciplined resolutely.

The Act of Taking Things Lightly
- A person who does not show up at a meeting place on time.
- A person who does not advance even after hearing the blast of a trumpet.
- A person who hides behind something and remains still, taking advantage of the fact that no one can see him.
- A person who stays close to his comrades at the beginning, but soon disappears.
- A person who fails to respond when his name is called.
- A person who is poorly armed and equipped.

These people must be disciplined.

The Act of Underestimating
- A person who fails to relay commands to others.
- A person who does not properly relay commands to others, creating confusion among soldiers.

- A person who pays no attention to a signal to advance or retreat, disregarding banners that symbolize the military.

The Act of Stealing

- A high-ranking officer who is careless about food and shows no appreciation for soldiers' hard work.
- A person who treats his subordinates unfairly and shows favoritism toward his friends.
- A person who arbitrarily takes away someone else's possessions. A person who does not return the things he borrowed from someone.
- A person who takes credit for someone else's achievement.

The Act of Deceiving

- A person who changes his name without permission.
- A person whose military uniform is filthy.
- Banners are in tatters.
- There is no signaling device such as a golden drum, which is used to instruct troops to advance or retreat.
- Swords are dull and thus useless.
- Feathers are missing from arrows.
- Bowstrings are not held in place on the bows.
- Soldiers disobey military commands.

The Act of Disobeying

- Soldiers do not advance even after hearing a trumpet blast.
- Soldiers ignore the order to retreat and keep advancing.
- Soldiers do not hunker down even when banners are lowered. Soldiers do not get up even when banners are raised.
- Soldiers avoid taking the lead and withdraw to the back of the unit.
- Soldiers break formation by acting haphazardly and lower the morale of the unit.
- Soldiers are ready to run away with no intention of fighting.

Soldiers are running about in confusion.
- Soldiers desert the front line under the pretence of rescuing the wounded or recovering the bodies.

The Act of Disturbing
- Soldiers act in a disorganized manner on the way to the battlefield, in a struggle to occupy the first position.
- Roads are brimming with tanks and mounted soldiers, limiting the mobility of the troops.
- Soldiers are yelling at each other, making it impossible for them to hear commands, which will disrupt the execution of commands.
- Soldiers are pushing and shoving at each other, disrupting the formation of marching troops and damaging their equipment and weapons.
- Soldiers from the top to the bottom are moving about randomly.

The Act of Leading Others in the Wrong Direction
- When stationed at the base, soldiers search for their fellow countrymen and socialize selectively with those close to them.
- Soldiers disregard martial law and sneak into other units without permission, ignoring the order to stop.
- Soldiers move from one unit to another through the backdoor without notifying their superiors.
- Soldiers cover up someone's wrongdoing and take responsibility for the act collectively.
- Soldiers get together to have a drinking party, promising to do each other a favor.
- Soldiers shout out "Enemy!" and agitate security guards.

Soldiers who engage in the above acts must be disciplined resolutely. Disciplinary action will ensure smooth operation.

Effective Strategy

Those who are responsible for governing a country must be able to meet current challenges while having a clear vision for the distant future. They may stumble if they do not pay attention to immediate challenges.

A wise man does not concern himself with his superior's responsibilities. You should perform your duties before concerning yourself about other people's affairs. You should tackle impending issues before strategizing for the future.

Major issues require complex solutions; minor issues require simple solutions. Do not take a one-sided approach to solve problems.

To make profits, you should take losses into account. If you want to succeed, you should also consider the possibility of failure. To reach higher ground, do not disregard the foundations at the bottom.

Focusing only on what lies ahead while advancing may result in failure. Danger arises from safety. Demise arises from existence. Chaos arises from order.

A wise man can anticipate what will happen next merely by detecting signs. He can predict the ending by looking at the beginning. This ability enables him to avoid unfortunate consequences.

Two-Dimensional Approach

To take a one dimensional approach is to take a myopic attitude; you are preoccupied with the present with no regard for the future. Conversely, you are preoccupied with the future with no regard for the present.

Things should be viewed in totality from two sides. Try to work with clear vision for the future as well as awareness of the current situation.

Do not give orders self-righteously. Do not look at issues sub-jectively, one-dimensionally, or superficially. Turn your eye and mind's attention to your surroundings. Try to look at the whole picture.

The cause of failure lies in the unwillingness to look at the whole picture. Giving orders self-righteously reflects a lack of ability to grasp the essence of things.

"If you know your enemy as well as yourself, you will easily win 100 battles" (Sun Tzu).

BOOK FOUR

The Nature of the Martial Arts

The nature of the martial arts is to bet the second most important thing, next to your life, to realize your life, and to make it meaningful as well as to improve it.

Life is limited and death is inescapable. To improve the quality of your life, you need to live with a sense of purpose. It's a challenge. Sutras can help improve the quality of your life.

Attitude Toward Training

The basic goal of martial arts is keeping the right attitude and applying the logic of martial arts for the society as well as for oneself.

The foundation lies in the mental and physical attitude. It's the seriousness that you see things thoroughly and correctly without being flattered by superficial glamour.

The aspiration is to practice the truth. The heart of people who have the vision has to be pure, soft, gentle, yet sharp. It is the action to leave your thoughts behind. Everything keeps changing. Train to coordinate the condition and grasp the essence under such transitional situations.

Discipline

In martial arts, you train to sharpen the five senses to understand emptiness (*ku*). The path will appear only after you understand esoteric learning using discipline.

The path is the way that corrects your mind and body. The path is called *Do* in Japan, *Tao* in China, and *Yoga* in India.

When you are young and full of energy, hone your skills and adjust your mind and body. When you get older, refine your wisdom without relying on your skills and adjust your mind and body. It is better that you are great yourself regardless of the skills and wisdom. There are age-appropriate ways to apply martial arts. Lack of the knowledge will destroy your mind and body.

In the teaching of martial arts, you can understand the world of emptiness and use it as a means to make a large step forward by training your body and opening the world of sutra mind.

Haki – *Haki* refers to ambition, energy to win, and enthusiasm to conquer others. Success means to accomplish *Haki*.

Those with *Haki* will advance and earn success.

Training of vital energy (Prana) – In martial arts, vital energy can be trained by bringing internal energy and external energy into the body.

External energy—positive (+, *yin*) is the energy of the sun that you take in during the day.

Internal energy—negative (-, *yang*) is the energy of night air that you take in at a cemetery at midnight.

Samskara of martial arts is a training to balance *yin* and *yang*. The purpose of the training is to attain happiness, longevity, health, and peace.

Human Nature

When we face a crisis, we are awakened to the possibility of seeing things from a different viewpoint and starting the process of regenerating and restructuring.

Take action believing that all possibilities are there as a challenge. You should be innocent, modest, and nimble for challenges.

The first step of practice is to exercise your vital energy and fully apply your personality. In order to do that, become aware of self-esteem and pursue a creative life.

When your heart is rich and flexible, you gain ability and are able to aim at the middle path.

Balancing introversion and extroversion clears your mind and produces refined theory and a rigorous ideal.

Extroverted

Extroverted refers to other people and the outer world. Extroverted people have amusing energy and are likely to be everybody's friend. They are open-minded and their hearts go outward.

Introverted

Introverted refers to focusing on oneself. Most of us tend to be introverted. When we experience setbacks and deadlocks, this tendency grows and our heart becomes reclusive. With your heart overcast and confined, you start to see more of your negative factors. By holding back your shortcomings, your action will change drastically.

Dealing With Your Introverted Self

Discover and recognize your plus side, and you will be more positive. Wake up to the nature of your personality. You will discover pride and joy and become more positive. Bring out the best of your potential and vital energy.

Review your ability from various angles. Recognize your ability and learn how to use it. Try to be mild-mannered yet be strong. Exert your energy outward strongly. Do not put a brake on your energy. Bearish attitude will cause you to miss opportunity. Gain toughness. Do not have likes or dislikes of people.

Do not judge people looking at their shortcomings. Judgment works against your vital energy. You will take the poison of others and impair your relationships.

Try to be positive. To take full advantage of yourself, look for a place to be jostled. Tackle with the work at hand earnestly. Do not be jealous of others. Do not feel inferior.

Do not escape, dive in. You will find development and growth of life there.

Rei-gi (*Etiquette*)

Cultivation of Ego

Any Genius Makes Mistakes.
Adversity starts from negative energy while the path is opened up for positive energy. Be generous to your own reality. Do not seek for perfection in competition. Those who take advantage of their opponent's mistakes win and those who are discouraged lose.

Fear
We all are afraid of something. Your mindset creates terror and angst. And the fear prevents your ability to take action.

Everyone in this world has something to fear. Courage defeats fear and resolves your angst. You are scared until you step into the fear. Once you are in it, feelings of fear disappear. Likewise, once the battle begins, all you can do is to take action and you don't have time to fear.

Those who are aware of their own fear are more devoted.

The more experienced you are, the more you see the depth of hardship both in martial arts and the workplace. If you stop feeling fear, you no longer have improvement or growth.

Do not be afraid of being nervous. Real gumption has its meaning in that you recognize it.

Passion
When you are young, you can challenge by taking a risk pushed by passion. We become more careful in middle age. Prudence calcifies your mind. In order to break the calcified mind, you need to cultivate fresh passion and build up the power to start again.

Goals have obstacles. In order to search for perfection, bring down the confidence of the past, awaken to new creations, and challenge the possibility of changing course.

Ideally, always have desire and passion. Have the strong passion of belief.

Application of Courage

When you step into an unknown territory, you notice that risk becomes real. You also realize that real risk causes innovation. When you are intimidated, development of your ability falls into decay.

New departure takes courage and patience. Repetition makes patience. It becomes a drive, and ability grows out.

Having intellectual modesty towards learning and eyes to look at others and yourself in relation to them, you can bring courage out of people. To do that, you must have courage to listen to others well, explain, and convince them, as well as courage and tenacity to outstand adversity.

Do not let people who are engaged in a plot come closer to you.

Thoughts

When you have pride and a clear target to accomplish, you work hard to the best of your ability, pouring your energy in to attaining the goal. To have confidence, you need to be free and have the ability to make an effort. For that, you need to hold yourself back and be able to give teamwork first priority. You also need to know the limits of your knowledge and ability well. You need to be bright, act on logic, be consistent, and have mature thoughts. A coward tries to hide the fact that he is scared. He is afraid of taking off his mask and becomes servile to the strong. You should be yourself at all times.

Sloppy people not only squirm but also are swamped with work. Many of those who cannot attain a goal are sloppy and they are often greedy and try to have all power at hand. People around them are perplexed and will be unable to support them.

Greed

Greedy people do not know the relationship between hardship and value. Most of those who are unaware of the relationship become prodigal and fall into contempt. Wealthy people teach their children to save money and preach that when they acquire something, they need to give up something in return.

Experience

People say that a man becomes full-fledged after turning 60 years old.

To form yourself, you need to struggle in reality and gain experience to make yourself tough and grow up. Theory and logic are hardly enough. Those who edge out the competitors and gain experience can seize a chance. People with strong vital energy are more likely to succeed.

Consider that everything, even hardship, will happen to you. You gain strong courage and vital energy from such experience.

Taking a Bet

When it comes to taking a bet, act like you have an iron hand in a velvet glove. Take a rigid stance when you work on an important issue. The true value of a person shows up in an important affair. Live your life with willpower and pride.

Life is a series of bets. Accept with a smile when you lose. This will give you a new drive.

Growth

Growth brings out your potential. Learn the lower load of the society until you reach 30. There is no world that does not embrace bitterness.

The contradiction and absurdity you experience working for people brings leadership out of you when you are in a leadership position. Do not keep the people you dislike away from you. True personality has to come naturally out of where your ego is refined and exercised.

Seek for a good mentor when you learn things. Bury your ego and learn with the guidance of a mentor; it's at the very bottom of that place where your true personality is born.

Do not try to be unique and creative from the beginning. Close your mouth and learn without a word. You become free and flexible only after you learn the form from your mentor; the creative frontier will then open up in front of you.

If you are unskilled, be armed with your honesty. Be loyal to your personality and talent.

There is always a wall before growth. Search for a way that suits you to break the wall. Be aware of your positive side. Be confident and devote the best of yourself.

To know your positive side, do not calculate. Be tough. Trust your ability. Be used to simple things. Be a reliable person. You must have honesty to be trustworthy.

Courtesy

Show an attitude of courtesy before the other person does to you. It makes sense that you bow first when you are with older or higher ranking people.

Even among friends, those who noticed first should show an attitude of courtesy. It is the manner that you do it before your mentor or senior superiors. There is no mentoring relationship without manners.

It is good manners in the martial arts to wear a white belt when you meet your new mentor to learn at another school.

Creativity

Creativity gives you courage. Do your best against contradiction and imperfection. Wake up to your ego.

Regeneration

Withdrawal from worrying about social status allows better regeneration to occur, which is different from the past. Regeneration refers to people who make living success and challenge their possibilities. To live, you need to step into the unknown transformations. There are willpower, self control, courage, patience, and inhibition at the bottom. It also takes inspiration.

Self control

Mental control takes power and passion. It requires strong force to control yourself. You always need to be calm on the battlefield.

People release tension at the moment when the battle is over and fall into a dangerous situation.

The Road of Learning

It must be blank at the starting point of teaching and learning.

Its farthest land is the world of the nothingness (*mu*) and the emptiness (*ku*).

Each of us has our own perspective. The difference between good and evil depends on the combination of perspective.

Mental Attitude of a Leader

- A leader should try to be fair. If you want to become a leader, try to become a mature person.
- Be flexible enough to play various roles.
- Try to be a leader who finds anything that makes each person number one and gives them confidence. Compliments give them a small goal.
- A leader leads people to positive thinking. Important things are invisible.
- Use words correctly. There is a saying "words make heaven."
- Try to give a refreshing greeting. When you greet, be positive and bright with warm heart hoping that the day will be meaningful.
- When you receive a greeting, do not swagger.

Do-ryoku (*Effort*)

Mindset of Martial Arts and Sutra

Our forerunners reached enlightenment risking the second most important thing next to their lives and made use of it in life. They advocated going back to nature and sought for reason, saying that it would be enough if they had enough food to survive and enough clothes to keep warm.

If you want to pursue training, you need a certain mindset. Realization refers to the state you acquired from mental and physical training and wisdom. It is believed that it's difficult to reach enlightenment just through knowledge from learning; the top priority in training is to realize through wisdom.

Stress
When we are under stress, we tend to be violent. Law and order are broken deliberately. To control your stress, lead your mental and physical balance to the middle path.

Courtesy (Rei)
To run a country, do it with courtesy. Make modesty your motto. Do not value wit and speech, but take action. The path is where sincerity and action are.

Courage
It is only natural that we try hard. Courage opens up the path wider. It is the courage that outraces genius.

Secret to continue
Make things simple. Be used to simplifying things. Simply feel confident. Grasp people simply. By simplifying your life, toughness, positivity, the ability to take action, and gumption will also come out.

BOOK FIVE

Mind Control and the Method

The Rules of Mystic Power

Facing Difficulties is Inevitable in Your Life
Difficulties are there for you to challenge. Difficulties are there to be your friends. When you face difficulties, listen to your heart and search for unlimited possibilities.

Go Back to Your True Self.
Always observe things. Observe how the mind works, observe vice and virtue in things. Apply those to your movement and start action.

Look Inside Yourself Before you Start Any Action
Look around the world. Something new will start from there.

The Beginning is Always Important.
The beginning is determined by how you prepare yourself.

People are Afraid of Making Mistakes, Afraid of Making Wrong Decisions.
You don't have to show fear to other people. You need to face your fear and you will be immunized. There is no shortcut.

The Hungry Spirit Will Take you in the Right Direction.
There is no secret to success. There are always problems as long as people exist and nature exists. You can always find chances in problems. *Keisho* shows you the way to live.

Miracle and Mental Preparation

In the martial arts, it is important to purify yourself mentally as well as physically. When you train and master your mentality and your skill, you have a chance to get a glimpse of the miracle world.

Energy Flow and Magnetic Field.
The land has cosmic power. Humans have the same kind of energy.

The place affected by magnet power is called the magnetic field. Magnetic energy has both good and bad kinds. Two magnetic fields can push each other and can be negated. When the power is negated, the magnetic fields can produce unknown energy.

When magnetic field and human energy push each other and turn into zero, it becomes something called zero magnetic field. When that happens, it is known that the field produces healing energy or supernatural effect.

The blood contains iron. Iron reacts to the magnetic field. The brain and body react to the electric signal. Electricity reacts to magnets. There is mystic power between the body and super natural events. Some people call this mystic unknown power the occult.

Water Vein
A water vein is a body of streaming, flowing water, and can cause strange effects. A water vein can produce electricity by rubbing small stones. When there is a water vein under the bed, it is known that the effect called Geopathic Stress causes bad physical condition, illness, and even death.

Dowsing
Dowsing is a way to find a water vein by sensing information from materials using sticks or pendulums. Some people get sick just by standing on a water vein.

Energy and Pore
The power of no obsession is acquired by relaxing the tension and uniting mentality and techniques. This power can be used as healing power. This is called a pore. There are types of people who can get benefit from pore and there are people who can't. There are two kinds of pore healings: One can cure a patient by working a pore directly to sickness. The other is to be patient and cure oneself.

The Brain and Memory System
When you remember something, you see a scene or an event that is sent to the nerves through the eyes and forms an image. The image becomes a signal. The information goes to the thalamus through the optic nerve and reaches the center part of the brain. It goes via nerve fibers at speeds of 250 miles (400km) per hour then reaches the neocortex.

The neocortex matches up the information with old memories. The information goes to the hippocampus where all the memories are stored. It is then determined at the hippocampus if information should be stored as a memory. Whatever is necessary to be remembered is recorded.

For a few weeks, the information in the hippocampus is stored separately in 50 different parts of the neocortex. When you remember something, all the separated pieces of information work together and replay.

Human Brains can be Categorized in Three Parts.
The brain stem is called the *brain of life*. It controls breathing and adjusts body temperature.

The limbic system is the home of the hippocampus that controls the memory and the amygdale that controls emotions.

The neocortex is called the *brain of intelligence*. It produces logical thinking. The brain of intelligence is categorized into two parts: the right brain which affects the arts, space, and recognition and the left brain which controls language, logic, and the ability to analyze.

The corpus callosum connects the right and left brains and exchanges information and works for recognition and behavior.

The Difference Between Women's Memory and Men's Memory

Women tend to be good at language recognition. Men tend to be good at space recognition.

Women easily store the memory of something that is strongly related to emotion. Women tend to remember their first sexual encounter more than men do. Women's brains tend to react more strongly to stimulus that causes strong emotions and remember it. It is because women's corpus callosum is twice as big as a man's.

A break up for women is hard not because of the fact of breaking up but because of the painful memory of the emotions involved in the breakup. Women can diminish old memories by experiencing new things. Women can diminish the memory of a painful break up by dating another man. Since women's corpus callosum is twice as big as men's, women recover from breakups more easily. Men, on the other hand, will hold on to the breakup longer.

Memory Function

Losing memories when you are drunk – Drinking too much alcohol can numb your hippocampus and neocortex which controls memories. Therefore, you can't store new memories. However, since you are still conscious and you have access to your old memory, you can still go home. On the way home, new memories can't be stored so you do not remember.

You don't lose your memories even when you get old – You don't lose your memories just because you get old. It depends on how you remember different things.

When one part of the brain is damaged – When one part of the brain that controls language is damaged, the other part gets more active. It could happen to anyone, for example, the part that controls vision could suddenly be released and empowered.

It depends on individuals how well memories are kept – Memories are controlled in hippocampus and neocortex for four years. These memories are not ready to be kept as long term memories yet. In rare occasions some children remember their past lives.

Brainwashing

Drugs were often used for brainwashing purposes in evil practices and ancient religion. Drugs were used to render someone unconscious and numb his entire body.

Drugs were often used in religion to lower the brain function and for brainwashing. This was used in ancient religions so that a shrine could keep its authority. The flowers gidacho and asagao were used to make drugs. They produce *dateyura*. *Dateyura* contains an alkaloid poison. Alkaloid poisons can lower brain function significantly. It can put a man in a half-dead condition. When you drop a special liquid on the half-dead person, he wakes up and panics. In the panicked brain, repeating the same objectives over and over can transform him into a slave.

There is detoxification that can wake up an unconscious person. It is liquid taken from the arubaru pea. The arubaru pea works as a detoxification for alkaloid poison (antidote).

Evil religious practices still exist. They take advantage of ignorant people and change them into slaves.

Placebos

Certain people can be affected by placebos (*The Placebo Effect*) and others cannot be affected.

Practice a real surgery on someone with a bad knee. Without actually practicing a surgery, practice an imaginary surgery on someone with a bad knee. The result is the same by making him believe he has had the surgery. This is called the placebo effect.

The power of awareness and belief works on the nerve system and heightens natural treatment. The patient himself functions as a medium to expel his sickness. Some kinds of energy substance are working inside. There are many unknown parts of this.

Developing Your Talent

To overpower other people and to overpower yourself, you need to analyze yourself so you can develop yourself. If you wish to develop your talent, learn the right basics and the right forms. You then need to find a teacher with great vision.

How to Develop Your Talent
1. Stay in good condition.
2. Have strategies and analyze for the next goal.
3. Observe your movements visually with video recording devices and analyze yourself.
4. Speak about the results of your analysis.
5. Train your rhythm. Listen to rhythmical songs and get your body used to them. Rhythmical sense is related to the cerebellum and nervous system.
6. You can restore your cerebellum by repeating what you did in the past one more time. You learn something by repeating. To repeat something patiently requires good rhythmical sense.
7. Wake your rhythmical sense.

The Principle of a Credulous Brain and an Incredulous Brain

When you hear someone talking fast, it increases your heart rate. It stimulates your sympathetic nervous system and also confuses your brain. The high tone of a voice has an impact on your brain. At first, you hear someone talking very fast and emphasizing some words with a high tone of voice. Your brain remembers the words spoken with a high tone.

Next, a different person speaks to you slowly. You tend to believe whatever the slow speaker says. That means you become easily deceived. After you are released from a tense atmosphere, you feel relieved and tend to believe people more readily than usual. The more you feel threatened by a tense atmosphere, the more you tend to believe people after the relief. This phenomenon is related to the functions of the sympathetic nervous system (which works to make you nervous) and the parasympathetic nervous system (which works to relax you). When the parasympathetic nervous system takes over from the sympathetic nervous system in your brain, you start feeling relaxed instead of nervous.

It is said that people ordinarily speak approximately 400 words per minute. If you are an ordinary person who speaks 400 words in a minute, your heart beats approximately 90 times per minute. This heart rate is normal. On the other hand, fast speakers are estimated to utter approximately 530 words, which increases the heart rate to 108, as fast as that of those who are nervous.

The brain has a mechanism to avoid being deceived. The front-orbital area in the brain instinctively produces a signal of doubt. However the function becomes dull when you are nervous. As a result, you tend to be trapped. You also have to be careful when you are under a lot of stress because your brain is lacking energy.

Methods to Create
an Incredulous Brain

1. Make fists with your thumbs inside, and you become difficult to deceive.
2. Doubt those who move their thumbs while speaking or apologizing.
3. Making fists with thumbs inside means sincerity.

Exercises such as walking are effective to create an incredulous brain, as leg exercises stimulate the front-orbital area in the brain. Children with credulous brains usually walk approximately 7,300 steps a day while children with incredulous brains walk more than twice that, 15,000 steps.

Rules of Things

Learning Method

The best way of learning something is to activate your brain while you are doing it. This method is effective in both learning and teaching.

Practice Method

Speak out loud. While speaking out loud, move around. When you move your body while speaking, it helps activate your brain. This is the best way to memorize something. When trying to memorize something, you need to voice what you are doing while you are doing it.

Be organized. Whether you are doing your work, study, or sports, it all depends on how you prepare. If you are prepared, you can get through everything. Being prepared means you have a certain procedure to follow. And establishing a certain procedure can be achieved by practice.

Learn how to practice organizing things. When you practice, be organized and write the procedure on a piece of paper. In order to obtain an advanced ability to organize things, you revise what you have written before, give a pause, and keep moving. When you organize something, it is important that you doubt the general representation first, then, get closer to the heart of the matter.

You can utilize cooking programs on TV to practice organizing. You can practice it by taking notes of the cooking procedure while you are watching it on TV. It is better to practice out loud.

Ability Development

The key to developing an ability to win against yourself and others is self-analysis. In sports, the form is a basic. If you want to develop your skills, learn proper basics. Look for a teacher with excellent foresight.

First of all, get yourself into good physical condition. Stay in good shape.

Make a strategy and an analysis for achieving your goal. Then analyze yourself by watching a video of your performance. In sports, tape yourself, check your movement and analyze yourself.

Put your analysis into words. Put your feelings into words. When you tell other people what you feel and what your goals are, you put yourself under pressure. That helps you to improve your skills.

Cultivate rhythmic sense. Rhythmic sense is related to the cerebellum and autonomic nerves. Degeneration of the cerebellum could be prevented by repeating what you have done before.

Repetition is the best way to learn something. In order to be able to repeat, you have to have a good rhythmic sense that enriches your mind and body. Have the patience to repeat.

Ability Development by Quick Listening

Quick listening means listening to something at a faster speed. By listening to high speed sound that is more than 2.7 times faster than the normal sound repeatedly, your following speed can be improved. As a result, you can bring your entire brain into action. The purposes of quick listening are to activate your brain and improve your diminishing memory retention and comprehension capacity.

Use a quick listening implement that enables you to play something four times faster and listen to it for 10 minutes per day. Listen to only something you are interested in.

First, listen at the normal speed, then raise the speed to two times faster, two-and-a-half times faster, and three times faster. A couple of months after you start quick listening, you will get used to the high speed sound and start to feel that your everyday conversation is slow. You will be able to predict what the other person is going to say next and that allows you to enjoy conversation freely.

Impressions That Sounds Give to Your Brain

Voiced Consonants – Men favor voiced consonants such as the "G" sound. That gives men an image of violence and makes them excited.

Children's Favorite Sound – The "P" sound is often used in the names of toys, kid's programs, and snacks. That is because the "P" sound gives your lips a good feeling when you pronounce it. You remember the feeling of your mother's breasts from your infancy and that gives your brain a good feeling.

Easing Sound for Women – The sounds of "N" and "M" give women feelings of comfort. They feel as if they are being held.

The Sound of "S" – This gives your brain a refreshing feeling.

Different sounds give people different expectations. Depending on their background and first language, the same sound has different meanings. Therefore, studying the relationship between sounds and people's perception is interesting.

Developing Ability by Training the Frontal Cortex

The frontal cortex governs organizing and scheduling skills. You should train yourself specifically to obtain these skills.

Start by cultivating the ability to mimic. In order to activate the part of brain which governs communications, you always have to put abstract things into specific words. In order to obtain the skills of scheduling and organizing, you need to practice until you can do it automatically.

Picture your goals and dreams. That gives you a driving force. Combine all these four approaches above to practice. This training method is also effective for infant education.

Wara-i *(Laugh)*

BOOK SIX

Humor and Laughter

Effective Use of Humor and Laughter

The body stiffens when it detects the sense of urgency. Laughter resolves stress and helps increase resistance against stress. A leader requires a sense of humor. Humor becomes a mind remedy and gives comfort for a moment. When you work, have fun and don't work too hard. Respond with humor against social systems, exchange ideas freely, and enjoy your sense of humor.

What is Laughter?
When you laugh, you are inhaling and exhaling deeply.

Short laughs are ideal. Short laughs put strong force on you, lift up your lungs, and heighten your diaphragm faster.

People laugh when tickled. It is said that oxygen intake doubles the deep breath resulting in three to four times higher than normal breathing during tickled laughter. When you are tickled and laugh, your oxygen intake is about the same amount as walking.

Our brain has mirror neurons that reflect the feelings of others. Infectious laugh is caused by this system. Mirror neurons are found in the frontal lobe. It reads the feelings from facial expressions and tone of voice and sends an order to make the same facial expression. This explains how infectious laughter and weeping in sympathy are produced.

Effects of Laughter
Laughter invites fortune (*fuku*). People who are laughing don't take a hostile view. Instead, they have positive feelings and even grow a sense of trust.

Laughter sets your mind free. You will have a positive attitude and gumption and nothing to fear. When you can laugh at yourself, you'll be a step closer to being the master of life, our predecessors said.

Earthy desires prevent us from having objective eyes. Do not be snagged on ambition, vanity, and desire, but laugh them off. When you get rid of a sense of shame, good things will happen.

You should laugh off things to see the joyous and delightful world. You can laugh off things because you love the world and people in it.

Human beings are frivolous animals. When you laugh, laugh off our ugliness, foolishness, and inconsistency.

The Playful Mind

Religious leaders say everything in life is for our training. Further to that, this world is a place of learning. You should, first of all, enjoy your playful mind.

We will eventually get tired. To avoid that happening to you, you should enjoy and create a space for your playful mind.

There is a proper attitude in a playful mind. Proper physical and mental attitude is: straighten your back, relax your shoulders, open up your chest, flow your power to the energy center, or *tanden*, and acquire the correct breathing method.

Right posture improves blood circulation and promotes health, and you will not lose yourself. Lean back and enjoy your playful mind. Saints valued balance and nurtured love.

Refining Your Spirit and Leaders

Things bother you less and less as they become habitual. The path will open up when you focus on making an effort to continue. It also helps protect your spirit.

It is impossible to settle matters ignoring one's interest and protect yourself from enemies. Only those who recognize the secrets of Mother Nature can handle matters. Understanding the bottom line requires knowledge and wisdom. Those who do not possess these elements are the same as being blind.

Knowledge (*chishiki*) is what you acquire through learning. Wisdom (*chishiki*) refers to the wisdom of the emptiness that naturally flows out of your heart. No one can teach you wisdom. You have to discern yourself.

Means
Means refers to the path to straighten your mind and body. Physical training, study and improvement of your technique will be the means to open up your supernatural power. It is good to be great and immeasurable when it comes to technique and mind. It will be a way to increase excitement.

Studying with vision can be a means to bloom your great ambition. Experience and mind training will be a way to open up your future.

Training for correcting your foolishness and training of self reflection will be the means to answer your calling.

Continue doing two things you don't like daily, and it will refine your soul.

Active Thinking
If you want to succeed in something, you should become fond of matters that accompany the thing and lead yourself to active thinking.

In order to lead to active thinking, go back to the basics and learn, apply, and think.

The Three States of Consciousness (*shiki*) aid judgments you make to enrich your life. Three states of consciousness refers to wisdom (*chishiki*), insight (*kenshiki*), and determination (*tanshiki*). The three states of consciousness are important factors to develop in life. We obtain wisdom, observe with insight, and make judgment with determination.

Temptation of Power

The art of war involves power. Power involves temptation and rituals. Where there are rituals, there is power.

When you sit in the seat of power, you need to be attentive to being humble and considerate—otherwise you ruin yourself and lose your position. Relationships with others will change when you look from the other person's viewpoint.

When people sit in the seat of power, they start to feel that nothing is impossible; they lose themselves and are manipulated by the temptation of power. Be aware.

Four Types of Power That Leaders Must Possess

The four types of powers are: power of observation, intelligence, determination, and brain power.

The essential qualifications that a leader must possess are leadership, planning, ability, global-mind, expectations, and cleanliness.

The essential qualifications that a leader must acquire are a suspicious mind, means of self protection, trustworthiness, and an aggressive instinct against enemies.

The essential qualifications of a hero are abundant knowledge, the power to make people obedient, great capacity, excellent determination, being considerate, excellent volition, and being rich in virtue.

Classification of Personalities Based on Sleeping Postures

Lying on One's Back with Limbs Outstretched – A person who lies on their back while sleeping with their limbs outstretched is uninhibited and tends to act in a self-centered manner (many children and celebrities are of this type). This person can be uncooperative, a poor listener, and likes to be at the center of attention.

Lying on One's Face – This person tends to be domineering and avaricious. He enjoys his life by avoiding the unexpected. This person is gregarious, self-confident, and anxious about his own affairs. Many wealthy people are of this type.

Lying in a Curled-Up Position – This person tends to be introverted and nervous. This person looks stern, but is actually friendly when engaging in conversation. This posture is common in stressed-out people. Many women are of this type.

Lying on One's Right Side with Knees Bent – This person usually does not have stress, has common sense, and is adaptable to society. This sleeping posture is healthy because it does not put an excess burden on one's internal organs; it also alleviates back pain. Holding a pillow horizontally to form the shape of an "S" while assuming this sleeping posture will distribute the muscle pressure evenly, resulting in reduced strain on lower back muscles.

Lying on One's Back – The person who sleeps in this manner is quiet and modest, but also self-disciplined.

Lying on One's Side with Hands Clasped as if in Prayer – This person looks open-minded, but is actually skeptical, sarcastic, and tends to be jittery as well.

Method of Identifying Body Types

Yang type (positive) are early birds. They are energetic in the morning and get tired in the evening. Their blood is sodium type. Their body type is dark skin with a small and firm body. Energetic. They are executive type of people and can drink alcohol and eat steaks in the morning. Their noses are often red.

Yin type (negative) tend to be in a bad mood when they wake up. Their brains don't work in the morning. Children with this type often collapse during the morning at school. Their blood is the potassium type. Their body type is such that they tend to get sick when they are children. Their ribs can be seen on their torsos. They are also executive type of people with big bodies. Even if they are energetic, they can easily develop anemia. Their body type is different from that of Yang type of people.

Judgment Based on Habits

An unconscious pattern of behavior that is acquired through frequent repetition is called a habit. A habit comes from the cerebral limbic system. A habit is an unconscious choice of the cerebral limbic system which seems like instinct.

How to Identify a "Mama's Boy"

If your head goes first when you put on a t-shirt, you may be a mama's boy. You still get dressed in the same way as your mother told you when you were a toddler. People usually start to put arms first as they grow, because it is simply more reasonable. But if you don't change your way, it means you still depend on your mother. These people tend to pass the buck to others. Since they are indecisive, they often call their mothers and depend on her decisions. They also go shopping with their mothers.

Habits of Hidden "Mama's Boys"

1. They have to sit down when they put on their shoes.
2. They bite a straw.
3. The room light is kept on when they go to sleep.
4. The door is kept open when they go to bathroom.

Identifying a Narcissist

Where in your mouth do you put your toothbrush first when you brush your teeth? If you go front teeth first, you pay careful attention to how you look. You like yourself and have too much self-confidence. You often check a mirror and touch your hair in order to make sure that you look good. You take a long time when you take a bath.

Judgment Based on the Way You Walk with Your Partner

When you try to see who is dominant in a couple, you can check which side a husband and wife are standing on and which hands are their stronger hands. If your partner is standing on the opposite side of your stronger hand, you keep your stronger side free. That means you want to control your partner. The person whose stronger hand is free is more dominant in the couple; when you both sit together; when you both are sleeping on a bed.

For example, if both a husband and wife are right-handed, if the woman is on the left and the man on the right, the man is more dominant. Conversely, if the man is on the left and the woman on the right, the woman is more dominant.

The exception to the preceding observation is if a woman is on the left side and holds a man's arm tight. She unconsciously wants to control the relationship. The man tends to listen to whatever she says. He tells her every important thing and she takes care of the household economy and makes final decisions.

Hidden Habits

If you hold a phone with your left hand, you tend to be stubborn. People who hold a telephone with their right hands are supposed to be flexible. If you often touch your face, you have a desire to transform yourself. If you often smell things, you tend to be always nervous.

Methods of Judging Handwriting

Handwriting indicates our current mental conditions as well as our original character.

Judgment based on Number 1
The number [1] identifies whether you have a supple mind or are stubborn. There are two types of handwriting and they are obviously different.

1. Drawing only a straight line for the number 1: [/]
2. Attaching a short stick to the line for the number 1: [1]

If you draw just a straight line for the number 1 you have a supple mind. Small shop owners at shopping malls tend to have this handwriting.

If you attach a short stick to the line for the number 1 you have strong desire to accomplish whatever you do. Researchers tend to have this handwriting.

[1] If you attach 2 sticks to the line for the number 1, you tend to stick to your own way of doing things. You have strong opinions and never give up. You may be so stubborn that you don't want to change your mind easily. You may eventually find yourself alone.

Judgment based on the Number 9
Considering the number 9, people write the circle part of the number increasingly smaller as we become older. As we age, we learn to be efficient. That's why the circle becomes smaller. The size of the loop in the 9 tells you whether you prefer being with people younger than you or older than you.

[9] If the diameter of the loop is larger than the line in 9, you

prefer being with people younger than you. You have a younger mentality. You like younger people.

[*9*] If the circle is small, you prefer being with older people. You don't like complications so you prefer being with tolerant older people.

An older person who writes a larger loop in 9 and a younger person whose loop is small tend to get along with each other.

Judgment Based on the Number 3
If you write the number 3 with a slant, it should be shifted straight when judged.

[*3*] Number 3 tells you whether or not you like being a leader in a group.

[*3*] If the lower line is longer than the upper one, you like organizing people. When you are working in a group, you want to manage the group.
If the lower line is shorter than the upper one, you tend to be modest.

Judgment based on the alphabet
How you write M and N indicates your way of thinking.

[*M*] [*N*] If you write the top part of M and N acutely, you are a quick thinker and capable of collecting information very fast. You are very quick.

[*M*] [*n*] If you write the top part of M and N roundly, you are a slow and logical thinker. Logical thinkers tend to write their letters roundly.

[*M*] If you write the right side of the top part of [M] bigger than the left side, you may be self-conscious.

Hormones and Personality

According to many scientists, it is hormones that determine one's marriage partner and control romance.

Women take pleasure in sharing and men like to be the best. The tendency of personality is affected by how much male hormone the baby is exposed to in the mother's womb. The amount of the hormone can be judged by looking at the length of the annular, or ring, finger.

Men with Long Annular Fingers

When a baby is exposed to more male hormone in the mother's womb, the baby will have long annular fingers. If the exposure is less, the fingers will be shorter.

Someone with long annular fingers is strong in the fields of science and mechanics and does not get swayed by others.

Men with Short Annular Fingers

Those who are not exposed to as much male hormone will be sensitive and are aware of people's feelings. Someone with short annular fingers can be successful as an actor and has great ability to attract people's hearts.

Testosterone

It is the male hormone that drives you into love. The hormone changes the mood of romance. Women tend to choose men who are genetically distant because of this love hormone. Pregnant women do not fall in love. The mothers will not be in the mood for love until her child becomes two years old.

Cold and Cough

Color of Phlegm

The color of phlegm helps distinguish the type of illness. Reddish phlegm (blood in phlegm) could indicate more serious illnesses such as lung cancer or tuberculosis. Greenish phlegm could indicate pseudomonas aeruginosa. Yellowish phlegm could indicate a severe cold or bacterial pneumonia. When whitish phlegm is present, asthma or COPD (chronic obstructive pulmonary disease) could be suspected.

During a severe cold the color of phlegm changes from yellowish to whitish as the condition recovers due to antibiotic, and other medications. It is the sign that the bacteria is disappearing.

Cough

It is said that one cough burns up 20 kcal of energy. If you cough five to six times in one hour, you will consume 100 kcal. This energy consumption is comparable to two hours of running.

When the cough lasts more than three weeks, it causes respiratory difficulty and may even lead to death. COPD (chronic obstructive pulmonary disease) could also be suspected.

Whooping cough is a severe cough that can cause your ribs to break and you may lose consciousness.

Cough can be divided into two types

1. Dry cough: Whooping cough when the cough lasts long, asthma
2. Wet cough: Pneumonia, chronic bronchitis.

Do not try to stop a cough. Coughing lets bacteria out of your system. We tend to cough more often during the nighttime. It is because the parasympathetic nerve (for relaxation) becomes active causing bronchial tubes to shrink.

Mycoplasma pneumonia has symptoms of high fever and

severe cough and is more common in younger people.

The theobromine contained in cacao is effective for a cough. 100g of chocolate that contains 70 percent or more cacao is recommended.

Do not take red pepper for a cough. The capsaicin in red pepper inflames the mucous membrane of the throat and makes you cough more.

Depression

People who are more likely to develop depression are:

1. *Perfectionist type* – He is bothered by small mistakes and wants everything done completely and perfectly.
2. *Dependent type* – He depends on others and wants to do everything by rule.
3. *Self-accusing type* – He thinks that every trouble around him/her is caused by himself.
4. *Selfless type* – He cares about others more and puts others ahead of himself.
5. *Order-oriented type* – He is well-organized. He cannot stand when things do not work out as he plans.

Those who can easily be caught by the above five factors tend to develop depression. There is a mechanism in depression where the patient tries to protect himself by acting positive. As a result, he mistakenly takes action to get free from stress.

BOOK SEVEN

Image Reading

Basic Information from Countenance and Figure

There is an observation method to speculate characteristics of illness from the countenance. This study became the basis of the method to make a preemptive move before the illness got worse.

Since ancient times people often said, "do not have energy, there's a shadow of death" and the reading became real despite the fact that there was no scientific proof. Why is it? Some of the methods of eastern physiognomy that are still alive today are derived from experience and facial reading.

Each of us has our own unique habits. Identifying these habits put us a step ahead.

Observation of the contour and body figure can be used as reference, but you cannot be obsessed with it.

Basic Body Figure From the Face

There are four basic body types: (1) brain type; (2) breathing type; (3) digestive type; and (4) muscular type.

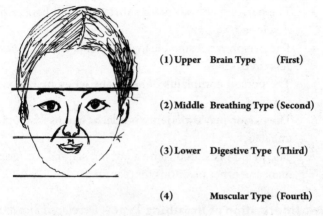

(1) Upper   Brain Type   (First)

(2) Middle Breathing Type (Second)

(3) Lower   Digestive Type (Third)

(4)   Muscular Type (Fourth)

The ratio of the Upper, Middle and Lower parts of the face is equal.

Basic Information of Brain Type

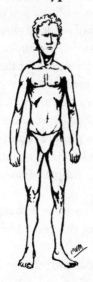

Inverted triangular-shaped face and dominant head

1. The person has a slender body.
2. The person has a wide forehead, slim torso, and slender limbs.
3. The person is physically insubstantial, but his brain is developed.
4. The person is not suitable for blue-collar labor. He easily gets tired.
5. The person complains of headache when he becomes sick.
6. The person may experience headache and psychological unbalance.
7. The person is suited to be a lawyer, scholar, congressman, and other positions for planning.

Basic Information of Breathing Type – *Developed face and chest*

1. The person is tall and slender and has wide shoulders.
2. The person has a thin chest.
3. The person's chin is obtuse and not angulated.
4. The person has hollow, long cheeks.
5. The distance between the pupils is relatively short.
6. Lungs are most developed for this person. It is better for him to live in an environment with clean air.
7. The person is very migratory.
8. Heavy mental labor without being able to exercise can cause the person physical damage. The person should take a walk and exercise to maintain health.
9. The person has a simple personality. He accepts strong points of others.
10. The person suffers from throat problems all year. The first symptom for the person when he becomes sick is throat ache.
11. The person has bad posture. He tends to stoop.

The person feels fatigue when he lives in unhealthy air and does unsuitable work. Too much fatigue may cause respiratory disease.

Basic Information of Digestive Type

Pyramid-shaped face. Lower part of the face is developed. In body, abdominal area is dominating.

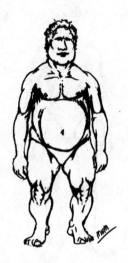

1.   This type is also called drinking and eating type and the lower area of the face is plump.
2.   The person has plump cheeks and lower jaw, and large mouth with thick lips.
3.   The person is apoplexy type.
4.   The person's corners of the lower jaw are developed and large with a sharp angle.
5.   The person's digestive apparatus and gastrointestinal areas are weak. Many have a potbelly and are overweight.
6.   The person has a good complexion and large volume of blood. The person a has reddish face.
7.   The person will be successful in cooking.
8.   The person is crapulous and vulnerable to gastrointestinal disease. The person has hearty appetite and is a big eater.
9.   The person is prone to developing diarrhea.

Basic Information of Muscular Type

Ratio of each part of the face (upper, middle, and lower) is equal. Also ratio of chest and abdominal area is equal.

1. The person is well balanced in every point in terms of the parts of the face.
2. The person projects the image of a boxy face.
3. The person's nose and chin are not very defined.
4. The person has a high and wide forehead.
5. The person has a square trunk and his figure is well balanced.
6. The person has long limbs.
7. The person has well-developed muscles and bones.
8. The person is suitable for muscular exercise and labor. This type is common in athletes.
9. Descendants of digestive type ancestors become muscular type. Nutrition intake and the work out of each body part will give them well-proportioned bodies.
10. The muscular type person can prevent disease by engaging in an occupation that moves constantly like salesperson.
11. This person must be active as he will be sick if he stays home all day lying down. The person tends to have troubles in joints and muscles. He is prone to lower back and shoulder pain.

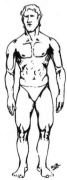

Basic Information of Combination Type

This is a combination of two or three types. This type can be identified from the symptoms when they get sick.

Taking advantage of strong points of each body type and compensating the downsides can help maintain health. We sometimes fail because of our strong points. We must not become overconfident and overestimate ourselves.

The Mystery of Money

Money has always supported one side of the art of war. Money has a mysterious dual nature. It grows people and their minds, but at the same time, it kills people. And yet, those who do not have desire for wealth are extremely rare in this world.

Kin-sen (*Money*)

The World of Money

You can see the true form of people behind money. People gather where there is money, and they drift away like the ebb of the tide when one goes bankrupt.

Attraction of money: Money can be a means to realize desire. When someone makes money, there is also someone who loses it.

Asset called oneself: Those who are good at making money still have the asset called "oneself" even if they lose everything. People in poverty are affected by a tyranny of wealthy people. They are likely to be deceived and oppressed.

In the world of money, wealthy people survive and become winners. Human beings are manipulated by deals designed by money. People never doubt that money could ever betray them. They believe that money is looking at them and are manipulated by it.

Where large amounts of money is involved, there is always a dark side. Those on the dark side crowd around the money and try to eat it up.

Really wealthy people are those who are well aware of the mechanism of interest rates. They loan money to poor people for high interest rates. Wealthy people have a thorough knowledge that money makes more money. Those who do not know this mechanism will be poor.

Saving money in a bank means that you lend money to the bank and the bank only pays the minimum interest.

People with money do not borrow money. Debt is always negative and never turns to positive. It is better being unhappy with money than being unhappy without money. However, spiritually affluent poverty surpasses both.

It is inconvenient if you do not have money. Money can make

you free. Doing business because of debt always fails. Some people say debt is also assets. Do not buy that opinion. It is foolish. If you want to minimize injuries in life, be aware that you are poor, take action for it, and strive to enrich your mind.

Mechanism of a Shoestring Operation

You are likely to fail when you try your hand at jobs for which you have little knowledge. You do not fall down when you are running desperately, but there is a limit.

When you have more than ten employees, it is beyond the sweep of one supervisor's eyes. You will need to hire more employees in order to increase sales. At the same time, labor cost and expenses also increase. And that's when financial transactions called shoestring operations begin. For a company to expand, you will need someone who can be your right hand. It is difficult to have competent human resources.

What is Social Reform?

In history, god and money—or religion and economy—are the causes of wars. Capitalists, religious people, and politicians share a mutual interest. They appreciate those who let them exploit. They appreciate those who are thankful even if the salaries are low. They appreciate those who thank God that they can eat every day.

By having them think that way, they exploit money from common people with God's authority. Capitalists, religious people, and politicians try to brainwash people to have them work obediently.

Human beings repeat history regardless of cultural climates, custom, and race. People at the bottom accumulate power by hoping for a new society and explode it. When they see contradictions in the society, the society is reformed and a new society is born.

Be conscious. It is the people who make changes.

Desire

Human beings have a weak point in that they are vulnerable to desire. People are weak against deals.

1. Deals have pitfalls.
2. When there is a man who sweats, there is another man who gains by the sweat.
3. You will be charged interest when you borrow money.
4. It will cause you a loss when you cannot see through the quality of goods.

On (*Small*)

Tai-ga (*Large River*)

Toku (*Virtue*)

Toku-jitsu (*Faithfulness*)

BOOK EIGHT

Wisdom Tactics

Wisdom of a Wise Man—Sontoku Ninomiya Goroku

In the late Tokugawa Shogunate period, there was a man who succeeded in several of the government's reconstruction works. He was respected by others as a wise man who saved the nation and was designated as the nation's greatest doctor. His name was Sontoku Ninomiya.

There are books that his pupils wrote, *Ninomiyaouyawa* (written by Masae Fukuzumi 1824-1892) and *Ninomiya Sensei Goroku* (written by Takayuki Saito 1819-1894) based on what they learned. The analects of Sontoku are integrated into these two books. The thoughts of Sontoku, who achieved great success in reformation, are highlighted in the next chapters.

The Wisdom of a Wise Man

Friendship

When a wealthy, talented, and well-educated person socializes with a poor person, he should not show off his wealth; when socializing with an untalented person, he should not show off his talent; when socializing with an uneducated person, he should not show off his education; when socializing with a person who is wealthy, talented, and well educated, he should devote everything he has to the relationship.

Make friends with someone's strengths but not his weaknesses. Merely eliminating one's ego is not sufficient. Reverence will be awarded only when you concentrate your mind and achieve a state of immobile mind where your mind is at rest. Actualize your life's potential, come to terms with your destiny, remove your ego, and venerate the immobile mind. *Hudo-son* (immobile reverence) means "Immobility is honorable."

Sheer Folly

When a torch has nearly burned up and its fire is drawing near your hand, throw it away immediately. When you are caught in a fire and are in great danger, abandon your personal possessions and escape. When a ship is about to sink due to a typhoon, cast the cargo away into the ocean. If the typhoon is still intense, break off the mast. A person who does not understand this line of reasoning is a sheer fool.

Bad Habits

It is difficult to transform someone who has acquired bad habits into a good person. Even if you reprimand him for his bad behavior, he will go back to his old habits. When teaching such a person, be careful and try to nip his bad habits in the bud. Failure to do so will cause his good habits to wither. Be patient and teach him the right habits over and over again. Associating with someone with base motives will destroy your life and your reputation. Associating with people of high standing will polish your rusty sword into a great sword.

Shortages
Your talents are finite, but your desire for luxury is not. People seek a life of luxury and few can live within their means. Even a powerful nation will suffer from shortages of goods unless people are willing to live in moderation. Such shortages cannot be supplemented.

A nation will prosper if it exercises moderation; otherwise, it will fall into poverty. A government may attempt to borrow money and squeeze money out of people merely to enrich itself. Such practice will surely plunge the nation into poverty. You need to have a firm foundation before you spring into action. A nation can rise from poverty if it repays its debts after establishing a secure footing and recognizing its limitations. Wealth can be amassed if resources are used sensibly.

Wicked People
Wicked people are like a sharp sword. When a wise leader makes good use of this sword, a nation will be governed effectively and people will be in peace. A nation under a foolish leader, who cannot make good use of this sword, will be governed poorly, leading to the suffering of people. By rejecting evil and utilizing righteous people, great achievements will be made. A righteous person can clearly see the negative qualities of wicked people, but not the negative qualities of righteous people.

This is because he inclines toward righteousness. In contrast, a wicked person can clearly see the negative qualities of righteous people, but not the negative qualities of wicked people. This is because he inclines toward wickedness.

A virtuous man will be heading in the right direction by associating with virtuous people. Likewise, an unwise person will be heading in the wrong direction by associating with unwise people. An unwise person tends to shy away from virtuous people. Such a person can be heading in the right direction by associating with virtuous people.

The Analects of Sontoku

A Poor Person

To rise from poverty and own a home, do not buy furniture or personal goods in large quantities. Borrow if necessary. However, you cannot break free from poverty if you continue to borrow. Work one day and buy with your money, because whatever you buy will be yours.

If a poor person tries to imitate a rich person without knowing his limitations, he will certainly destroy himself. If you want to emulate a wealthy person, live within your means and lead a frugal life to build up your wealth. If a poor person builds a house with borrowed money, interest payments may drive him back into poverty. This happens because he forgets about his poverty, overindulges himself, and fails to reflect on the miserable consequences of his behavior.

You will attain happiness by performing good deeds. You will attain virtue by being charitable and generous. You will lose virtue by accepting charity and generosity from others. If you attain virtue, you will have a family; if you lose virtue, you will ruin yourself. You should repay others for their virtuous acts by being virtuous yourself. Otherwise, your happiness will remain in yourself and will not benefit your offspring.

Ungratefulness is the source of destitution. Gratefulness is the source of prosperity and happiness. Ungratefulness will result in deterioration of your diet and clothing, perpetual conflict within your family, animosity, loss of friends, and eventually, destruction of your family. Do not forget to be thankful for the world and favors from others for even one day. Frugality may appear foolish, but will always lead to success. Extravagance may appear prudent, but will always lead to failure.

If your mind is focused on a frugal life, you will become rich.

If your mind is focused on a lavish life, you will become poor. Cook rice in a small amount; if that is not enough, cook some more. This is the right way to bring prosperity to your family. Similarly, this is the right way to bring prosperity to the nation.

Wait for ten days before buying a piece of fabric even if you have enough money. Wait for ten days before making clothes out of the fabric. Wait for ten days before wearing the new garment. You will flourish if you adopt this type of attitude.

No one can walk by taking two steps at a time. Our physical strength may vary, but everyone walks by taking one step at a time. You will fall to the ground if you try to walk by lifting both feet. Taking one step at a time is the only way to embark on the right path.

Gratitude
Always repay someone for his favor, and you can have everything your own way. If someone offers help without any compensation in return for your past favor, praise his act regardless of the circumstances. Show deep appreciation for his help. Give him a gift when he leaves. That is the right way to treat your friend. Express your gratitude even for a simple act of kindness. Such is the right attitude.

Public Office
A public office holder can accumulate wealth during prosperous times. But those are the times when one needs to treat others with the utmost respect and humbleness. If you have done that, no one will criticize you for enjoying yourself and living in luxury after retiring from public office. People will not be envious of your status. Working industriously while on active service and enjoying your life after retirement are equivalent to working hard by day and resting by night.

The opposite of this will incur people's resentment, and peace will not be maintained. Miseries and misfortunes will result.

Respectfulness is something that should be valued. Life can alternate between prosperity and adversity.

You cannot escape from this fact of life. When you encounter hardship, keep your head cool and take your time in dealing with it, as if you are coping with an afternoon shower. Otherwise, you will never be able to accomplish a goal.

Great River
A great river originates from small springs. As tributaries form a larger river, the width of the river widens. Likewise, cultivation of wasteland starts with one stroke of a hoe. Such small efforts will eventually open up a vast tract of wasteland. A wise person knows this fact very well, but a foolish person does not.

Happiness and Unhappiness
Happiness and unhappiness are two sides of the same coin. Something inconvenient to us is called unhappiness and something convenient to us is called happiness. Accept the fact that you are busy and be patient, and you will have some spare time in the future.

If a poor person is living under the care of a rich person, his family will eventually perish. Things always entail adverse effects. Wealth comes with the adverse effect of extravagance, while poverty comes with the adverse effect of idleness. Turn extravagance into frugality and humbleness; turn idleness into diligence. By doing this, the nation and people will be in peace.

After sowing the seeds of tranquility, you can enjoy watching them sprout, grow, and mature. If you harvest and eat the crop, your body will relax and your mind will rejoice. This is true tranquility.

Those who devour others' food and sake are useless for the nation. Those who like to go drinking at someone's expense are not good enough to be your confidant. When you do something with the intention of influencing someone's action, you will be lost without even being aware of it. This is as if a cabbage vendor removes dirt from cabbages to make them look different from their natural state in the field.

Everything should be done at the appropriate moment. Even if you are endowed with talent, eloquence, and wisdom, you will be able to use them only at the right moment.

Patience is the only way to go. The right moment is certain to come. Just like when you are rolling or unrolling a scroll, know exactly when you should act or keep a low profile. Otherwise, you will miss your opportunity.

Object of Comparison

Once a leader succeeds in establishing a nation, the right path is to turn his attention to the welfare of the people. This path should be compared to nature rather than oneself. If it is compared to oneself, one will fail to make great achievements that will lay the groundwork for future generations; moreover, one is likely to take a myopic approach that focuses on short-term results. Consequently, one may end up on the wrong path.

But if the right path is compared to nature, one will attain everlasting success. Do not sidestep complicated tasks that pave the way for future generations. Do not emulate a shortsighted person.

Virtues of a Virtuous Man

If a virtuous man behaves with humbleness, suppresses his pride, leads a frugal life, and helps the poor with his money, people will be impressed by his conduct and their resentment will be dispelled. People will be willing to work hard, feel no shame to wear shabby clothes and eat plain food, and enjoy living within their means. Overcome yourself, and you will be able to live modestly; conquer your selfish desires, and you will reap the benefits.

It is virtuous for a wealthy leader to merely wear shabby clothes. Such an act will dissipate the bitter feelings among the poor. Be generous and helpful to the needy, and you will attain virtue. Conquer your selfish desires and treat others with respect, and your field will be covered with an abundant crop that will lead you to virtue.

How to Carry Out Punishment

There is a saying, "Crows pluck at a field every time a farmer finishes planting." Such birds must be chased away once every three times. If you can punish and remonstrate wrongdoing from time to time and prevent people from committing misdeeds, you will be able to endure the duty of governing a country.

Even if a minister embezzles some money from the state coffers, the amount of the loss will be limited. However, extortion of taxes will destroy the common people, and the source of tax revenues will be lost forever.

Courage of a Compassionate Man

The courage of a compassionate man is flexible and strong. This is why people support him. The courage of a bold man is like steel. It is strong, but inflexible. This is why people do not support him. Flexible people tend to be too yielding. Being amenable and steadfast at the same time is the virtue of moderation.

A virtuous man likes to carve out a great path; an unwise man does not. Preaching a great path to an unwise man is useless. Neglecting your duty will reduce your worthiness as a person; performing your duty will enhance your worthiness as a person. A house will not exist without construction. Everyone in this world must work hard to fulfill their duty.

Sincerity

Those who seem calculating will always fall into poverty. Those who seem foolish can become wealthy, because they are not as foolish as they appear to be. The reason for their success is sincerity. A talented person without virtue cannot be a ruler. A talented, virtuous person without high standing cannot be a ruler. A prominent, knowledgeable monk with talent and virtue cannot be a ruler. Only a king can be the ruler of a country.

Flattery

A self-proclaimed allegiant offers advice that is pleasing to his master to curry his favor. His words may sound loyal, but are actually flattering. Such a person is greedily trying to win his master's favor and support and is likely to cause trouble for his master. A virtuous man should not have likes and dislikes.

A Boat and Water

Water makes it possible for a boat to float. But water can also overturn a boat. This is because waves have motion and non-motion. If you know the motion and non-motion of waves and how to manipulate a boat, your boat will not be overturned.

Those who build a fortune know how to manage their personal finances in response to the ups and downs of life. The path of the nation is created by people's actions. The law of the nation is created by people's deeds. The rules of the nation are created by people's words.

Success and Failure
Your success and failure depend on timing, and can happen quickly or slowly. The only thing you can do is to wait for an opportunity to come. Do not worry about something that has not matured; rather, utilize something that has fully matured. Finish something familiar, and then move on to something unfamiliar. Do something easy, and then move on to something difficult. People tend to fret over something that has not matured without paying attention to something that has already matured. Such is human nature.

If your efforts are focused on something you like, you will have to deal with something you do not like later on. If you are haughty, you will be poor. If you are frugal, you will be rich. You should not be fastidious about what you like and dislike. A person who relies on charity is idling away his time by waiting for help, with no intention of helping others. The universe has its own way. People have their limits.

Once people recognize their own limitations, the path to concession is created. Individuals, nations, and the world will inevitably decline without making a concession. Everyone will invariably perish if moderation is not observed. Endorsing others while stepping aside will pave the way for the establishment of your business. Exercising moderation will pave the way for the accumulation of wealth.

Whether or not this rule is observed will determine the nation's destiny. Moderation arises from diligence and idleness, concession and exploitation, poverty and affluence, rise and fall, order and chaos, and existence and non-existence.

Exercising self-restraint while knowing one's limitations represents diligence. Accumulating wealth by exercising self-restraint represents thriftiness. Using surpluses for the benefit of others represents concession. Concession will lead us to prosperity. When a nation prospers, peace will arrive, resulting in the nation's perpetual existence.

Ignoring self-restraint while knowing one's limitations represents negligence. Creating shortages by ignoring self-restraint represents wastefulness. Taking advantage of others to compensate for the shortages represents exploitation. This will lead the nation into disorder and destruction.

The rise and fall of a nation occurs naturally and this cycle repeats itself. To protect the nation from the danger of this cycle, *chu-yo* (the golden mean) must be practiced. By balancing out prosperity and decline, and poverty and affluence, the golden mean will be attained.

The nation will be governed effectively through observation of the golden mean. *Chu* (center) signifies the right path while *yo* (middle) signifies the law of nature. Accepting the law of nature and following the right path will bring order to the nation.

Quantity

Both nature and humans have a predestined role in the world. Acting within one's own limitations forms the basis of one's life. In so doing, the right path should be followed.

This means that one should lead a life of temperance by exercising self-control.

Here is how to live a life of temperance. Divide your income into four equal portions, use three-quarters of it, and save the remaining one-quarter. Here is how to use the three quarters of your income. Divide it by twelve to calculate how much you can spend each month. Furthermore, divide the monthly allocation by thirty to calculate how much you can spend each day. This is how you save money. In three years, you will accumulate one year's worth of savings, in nine years, three years' worth of savings, and in thirty years, nine years' worth of savings.

If a nation has nine years' worth of reserves, it can rescue people from hunger in the event of a poor harvest, drought, or flood. Nature sometimes wreaks havoc on people. It is certain that a disaster will strike within a few years.

One year's worth of reserves can be used to deal with a small-scale disaster. Three years' worth of reserves can be used to cope with a large-scale catastrophe. Even if there are no disasters, warfare may break out. Without sufficient funds, people will suffer under heavy taxation, and consequently, will grow apart. The nation cannot be sustained if it lacks the resources to support the public servants and common people.

Without nine years' worth of reserves, the nation is in need of money. Without six years' worth of reserves, the nation is in a crisis. Without three years' worth of reserves, the nation cannot be sustained.

If a merchant with a fund of $100 manages to run his business with only half the amount and keeps the rest of the money for other purposes, he will unwittingly accumulate inexpensive products, and will eventually make a profit.

Select certain items from your store and sell them at original cost, and you will make a great deal of profit. This is the trick of doing business. If the quality of the product exceeds its price, people will stop to take a look. Real profit comes from areas where profit is least expected. Businesses that may appear lucrative do not necessarily generate real profit.

Skills of a Wicked Person

A wicked person excels in intelligence and speech. He is well informed about what is going on in the world, from top to bottom. With his skills, the wicked person acts as an intermediary to solve a problem he himself has created deliberately. This is how he rakes in profit. Being unaware of his real intention, other people appreciate his help. This is a big mistake that may result in the downfall of the nation.

Plain Diet

Nothing will be accomplished until you have reached a state where you are so used to eating plain meals that you no longer crave lavish food. A person who prepares food for tomorrow after eating a meal understands the importance of preparing for the future. This understanding is necessary for the right path.

Application

A scholar may give a detailed lecture on books, but he does not know how to put his knowledge to practical use. Such a person is no different from a monk who recites a sutra. Knowledge is useless unless you know how to apply it to your daily life.

Thriftiness

Everyone assumes that money naturally goes to affluent people. But in reality, money accumulates in the hands of thrifty and hardworking people.

When people with earnings of $100 live on $100, no gap in wealth will be created. However, when they live on $80, wealth will accumulate; when they live on $120, wealth will vanish.

There is a difference between acting beyond one's capabilities and acting within one's capabilities. It is important to understand this distinction in order to act in a rational manner. Self-training should be done while you are still unsure of its usefulness. You will come to appreciate the value of the training later in your life.

ACKNOWLEDGMENTS

This is the third book of the "Secret Tactics" series.

In this book, I summarized two of the most famous Chinese classics and also focus on the wisdom tactics, which is thought to have influence on Chinese classics and their utilization.

Exceptional strategies developed by commanders who lived in the Age of the Warring States are still effulgent to this day without getting antiquated.

In the first book of the series, *Secret Tactics*, I shed light on the seven major types of swordplay and wrote on how ancestors lived out their lives making the most of the state of enlightenment.

In the second book, *Mind Power*, I made a complete and liberal translation of the Heart Sutra, a sacred book that explains balance of mind, body, technique, and reason in one-on-one situations and *Ku* (nothingness), and the search for a better state of mind.

I would like to encourage you to read through this series from the first book.

To write this third book I received an undue amount of encouragements and warmest support from many people.

I would like to thank especially Hisao Obata Sensei, Hitoshi Nishitani Sensei, Masami Tsurouka Sensei, and Tamotu Isamu Sensei, who gave a wonderful endorsement to this book. I also would like to thank Kyoji Kasao Sensei and Misako Kinoshita Sensei for generously providing a considerable amount of material for this book.

My gratitude is also to the following people for providing their great talents in each field. I would like to thank you to all with this book.

Translation
Junko Kamei, Maiko Hirai, Hiromi Kumasaki, Kaede Uji, Kazu Uji, Tse Hwang Yong, Tomomi Aozono, Hiroshi Minato.

Proofreading
Thomas B. Shea, Kanae Kolhi, Jeremy Chassen, Jared Chassen, Arielly Chassen, Deborah Chassen, Melissa Briscoe, Popsi Narasimhan, Zinger Yang, Paget Wharton, Jim Ambrose, Harold Gold, Dov Goldstein, Melt Bucholtz, Mattew Levin, Malte Loos, and Katushiko Naruoka.

Drawings
Mark Marttelli.

I would like to acknowledge these people for their exceptional support: Chales J. Garzik, Nicholas Christakis, William Chamberlin, Grover Boxley, Bruce Levy, Sandy Rosner, Ken Nishitani, Noritoshi Gondai, Jim Titosky, Koichi Mano, Katsuhiko Maruoka, Cosmo Capobiano, Bob Perrin, Jordan Berry, Bob Harb, George Noon, Dave Demori, Baba Tozu, Bill Chares, Ted Fowler, Andrea Tondo, Roberto Jaime, Reiko, Yuya & Takayuki Tabata, Fumiaki, Hironari & Yukari Kinoshita, Hitomi & Michiyasu Tamura, Yusaburo & Michi Miyashita, Kenko & Yoshimi Maruoka, Curtis Bee Wang, John Shirley, Richard Sheehan, Fusajiro Takagi, Ashi Yahola Somburu, Stan Keith, Brian Neltres, Sally Gorell, Koichi Mano, Mr. & Mrs. Koji Kuwabara, Mr. & Mrs. Sawa, Mr. & Mrs. Nagura, Joe Costa, John Costa, Cosmo Nadella, Anna Pelevin, Mr. & Mrs. Roman Pelvin, Mr. & Mrs. Kodama, Toma, Satomi & Koji Tsujimoto, Shoko Kimura, Mr. Shiomitsu (England), Vernon Simon, Mike Luce, James Morrow, John Hwee, Dan Cheron, Eymaro Riel, Fritz Kerr, Greg Cumming, Jhan Vacca, Julie Blencowe, Gayle Yoshimoto, Yutaka Baba, Lloyd Webbe, Ikuko K. Burns, Billy Conigliaro, Tony C., C. J. Hunt, Kimiteru Nakajima, Rich C., Joe Laquidara, Michael Inna Byrnes, Debra Martinez, Hiroaki Tabata, Fusako Tanaka, Yoshito Tabata, Eda Kinoshita, Tsuzumi Tabata, Momi

Imatsuji, Hiromi Tabata, Saneyoshi Tabata, Beverly Thomas, Mika Koh, Mr. & Mrs. Matsuyama, Baba Tozu, Shigeaki Nariai, Fukae Kazunori, Kumiko Fukae, Takako Nariai.

Gasshou
Kazumi Tabata

REFERENCES AND ORIGINAL CITATIONS

Nakamura Hajime, 2003. *Han Nya Kei Ten,* Tokyo Shoseki

Nakamura Hajime, 2003. *Hot Ke Kyo,* Tokyo Shoseki

Nakamura Hajime, 2003. *Jyo Do Kei Ten,* Tokyo Shoseki

Nakamura Hajime, 2004. *Ron Sho Ho Ka,* Tokyo Shoseki

Nakamura Hajime, 2003. *Yui Ma Kyo, Sho Man Gyo,* Tokyo Shoseki

Nakamura Hajime, 2003. *Kegon Kyo, Ryo Ga Kyo,* Tokyo Shoseki

Kino Kazutoshi, 1981. *Han Nya Shin Gyo Wo Yomu.* Kodansha

Masuda Hidemitsu (Hen Shu Cho), 2001. *Shaka No Hon,* Gakashu Kenkyu Sha

Masuda Hidemitsu (Hen Shu Cho), 2001. *Nich Ren No Hon,* Gakashu Kenkyu Sha

Masuda Hidemitsu (Hen Shu Cho), 1992. *Shin Do No Hon,* Gakashu Kenkyu Sha

Masuda Hidemitsu (Hen Shu Cho), 2007. *Shingon Mitkyo No Hon,* Gakashu Kenkyu Sha

Tachikawa Musashi, 1998. *Mitkyo No Shi So,* Yoshikawa Kobukan Inshinara Dai Do.

Masuda Hidemitsu (Hen Shu Cho), 1992. *Mit Kyo No Hon,* Gakashu Kenkyu Sha

Masuda Hidemitsu (Hen Shu Cho), 1994. *Koshin Do No Hon,* Gakashu Kenkyu Sha

Masuda Hidemitsu (Hen Shu Cho), 1993. *Shugen Do No Hon,* Gakashu Kenkyu Sha

O-Mori (Hen Shu Cho), 1992. *Do Kyo No Hon,* Gakashu Kenkyu Sha

Asakawa Yoshitomi, 2008. *I Nori No Shima,* Okinawa Kudaka

The Tuttle Story: "Books to Span the East and West"

Most people are surprised to learn that the world's largest publisher of books on Asia had its humble beginnings in the tiny American state of Vermont. The company's founder, Charles Tuttle, came from a New England family steeped in publishing, and his first love was books—especially old and rare editions.

Tuttle's father was a noted antiquarian dealer in Rutland, Vermont. Young Charles honed his knowledge of the trade working in the family bookstore, and later in the rare books section of Columbia University Library. His passion for beautiful books—old and new—never wavered throughout his long career as a bookseller and publisher.

After graduating from Harvard, Tuttle enlisted in the military and in 1945 was sent to Tokyo to work on General Douglas MacArthur's staff. He was tasked with helping to revive the Japanese publishing industry, which had been utterly devastated by the war. When his tour of duty was completed, he left the military, married a talented and beautiful singer, Reiko Chiba, and in 1948 began several successful business ventures.

To his astonishment, Tuttle discovered that postwar Tokyo was actually a book-lover's paradise. He befriended dealers in the Kanda district and began supplying rare Japanese editions to American libraries. He also imported American books to sell to the thousands of GIs stationed in Japan. By 1949, Tuttle's business was thriving, and he opened Tokyo's very first English-language bookstore in the Takashimaya Department Store in Ginza, to great success. Two years later, he began publishing books to fulfill the growing interest of foreigners in all things Asian.

Though a westerner, Tuttle was hugely instrumental in bringing a knowledge of Japan and Asia to a world hungry for information about the East. By the time of his death in 1993, he had published over 6,000 books on Asian culture, history and art—a legacy honored by Emperor Hirohito in 1983 with the "Order of the Sacred Treasure," the highest honor Japan bestows upon non-Japanese.

The Tuttle company today maintains an active backlist of some 1,500 titles, many of which have been continuously in print since the 1950s and 1960s—a great testament to Charles Tuttle's skill as a publisher. More than 60 years after its founding, Tuttle Publishing is more active today than at any time in its history, still inspired by Charles Tuttle's core mission—to publish fine books to span the East and West and provide a greater understanding of each.

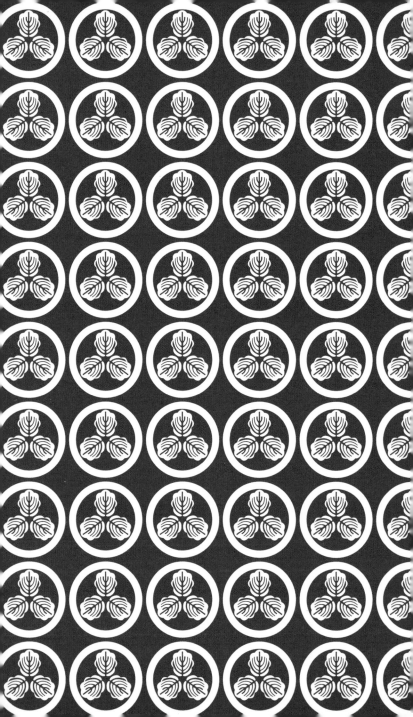